CAMBRIDGE MUSIC HANDBOOKS

Mendelssohn: *The Hebrides* and other overtures

CAMBRIDGE MUSIC HANDBOOKS

GENERAL EDITOR: Julian Rushton

Cambridge Music Handbooks provide accessible introductions to major musical works, written by the most informed commentators in the field.

With the concert-goer, performer and student in mind, the books present essential information on the historical and musical context, the composition, and the performance and reception history of each work, or group of works, as well as critical discussion of the music.

Other published titles

Bach: The Brandenburg Concertos MALCOLM BOYD
Bach: Mass in B Minor JOHN BUTT
Beethoven: *Missa solemnis* WILLIAM DRABKIN
Beethoven: Symphony No. 9 NICHOLAS COOK
Berg: Violin Concerto ANTHONY POPLE
Chopin: The Four Ballades JIM SAMSON
Handel: *Messiah* DONALD BURROWS
Haydn: *The Creation* NICHOLAS TEMPERLEY
Haydn: String Quartets, Op. 50 W. DEAN SUTCLIFFE
Janáček: *Glagolitic Mass* PAUL WINGFIELD
Mahler: Symphony No. 3 PETER FRANKLIN
Mozart: The 'Jupiter' Symphony ELAINE SISMAN
Musorgsky: *Pictures at an Exhibition* MICHAEL RUSS
Schoenberg: *Pierrot lunaire* JONATHAN DUNSBY
Schubert: *Die schöne Müllerin* SUSAN YOUENS
Schumann: Fantasie, Op. 17 NICHOLAS MARSTON
Sibelius: Symphony No. 5 JAMES HEPOKOSKI
Strauss: *Also sprach Zarathustra* JOHN WILLIAMSON
Stravinsky: *Oedipus rex* STEPHEN WALSH

Mendelssohn:
The Hebrides and other overtures
A Midsummer Night's Dream
Calm Sea and Prosperous Voyage
The Hebrides (Fingal's Cave)

R. Larry Todd
Professor of Music
Duke University

Published by the Press Syndicate of the University of Cambridge
The Pitt Building, Trumpington Street, Cambridge CB2 1RP
40 West 20th Street, New York, NY 10011–4211, USA
10 Stamford Road, Oakleigh, Melbourne 3166, Australia

First published 1993

A catalogue record for this book is available from the British Library

Library of Congress cataloguing in publication data

Todd, R. Larry.
Mendelssohn, *The Hebrides* and other overtures: *A Midsummer Night's Dream,
Calm Sea and Prosperous Voyage, The Hebrides (Fingal's Cave)* / R. Larry Todd.
p.   cm. – (Cambridge music handbooks)
Includes bibliographical references and Index.
ISBN 0 521 40419 3 – ISBN 0 521 40764 8 (pbk)
1. Mendelssohn-Bartholdy, Felix, 1809–1847. Overtures.
2. Overture. I Title. II. Title: *The Hebrides* and other overtures.
III. Series.
ML410.M5T64 1993
784.2' 18926' 092–dc20   92–36005 CIP MN

ISBN 0 521 40419 3 hardback
ISBN 0 521 40764 8 paperback

Transferred to digital printing 2002

Contents

Preface

Music historians have long recognized the concert overture as a genre in which Mendelssohn made a signal contribution. Though *The Hebrides* and *A Midsummer Night's Dream* retain a preferred status as his most frequently performed overtures, for several reasons they should be considered together with the *Calm Sea and Prosperous Voyage* Overture, thereby forming the group of three overtures treated in this volume. All three works were conceived or composed during Mendelssohn's student period of the 1820s, and indeed all three intermittently occupied his best efforts until well into the 1830s. Mendelssohn himself viewed the three as a coherent group: he deliberately withheld their publication in full score until 1835, when he finally allowed Breitkopf & Härtel to release the three together as *Drei Concert-Ouverturen*. Despite their disparate subjects – a Shakespeare play, two short poems of Goethe, and impressions of the Hebrides – the three reveal a commonality of stylistic approach to form, tonal planning, thematic transformation, orchestration, and treatment of programmatic ideas. The present study is intended to explore the relationships among the three works by considering, in turn, their rather complex geneses, their stylistic sources, formal structure, programmatic conception, and orchestration, and, finally, their influence and reception in the nineteenth century.

In preparing this study the author has incurred several debts to colleagues, students, and the staff at Cambridge University Press. In particular he wishes to thank Prof. Julian Rushton, the series editor of the Cambridge Music Handbooks, for his advice and counsel during the preparation of the manuscript. Prof. Rushton and Prof. Wm. A. Little of the University of Virginia offered several suggestions for the improvement of the volume; John Michael Cooper brought to my attention some important contemporary reviews of the overtures; and Isabelle Bélance-Zank carefully proofread the manuscript and prepared the index.

To my beloved daughter Anna Sophia, who arrived, with a special magic of her own, during the final stages of writing, this volume is affectionately dedicated.

October 1992

I

Background

Mendelssohn's concert overtures have always ranked among the most enduring staples of the nineteenth-century orchestral repertoire, a position conceded by even his staunchest critics. Richard Wagner, no slight disparager of Mendelssohn's music, viewed *The Hebrides* Overture as the 'masterpiece' of a 'landscape-painter of the first order';[1] and George Bernard Shaw, who took Mendelssohn to task for his 'kid glove gentility, his conventional sentimentality, and his despicable oratorio mongering', could only report glowingly in 1892 about the *Midsummer Night's Dream* Overture: 'The most striking example I know of a very young composer astonishing the world by a musical style at once fascinating, original, and perfectly new, is Mendelssohn's exploit at seventeen years with the *Midsummer Night's Dream* Overture. One can actually feel the novelty now, after sixty-six years.'[2]

Along with *Meeresstille und glückliche Fahrt* (*Calm Sea and Prosperous Voyage*, Op. 27), *A Midsummer Night's Dream* (Op. 21) and *The Hebrides* (Op. 26) were conceived during Mendelssohn's student period of the 1820s and mark the culmination of his early efforts to make a decisively original contribution to orchestral music. *A Midsummer Night's Dream* dates from August 1826, less than a year after the completion of the extraordinary Octet (Op. 20) in October 1825, a period during Mendelssohn's sixteenth and seventeenth years that surely must count as the *annus mirabilis* in his development and maturation as a composer of the first rank. *Calm Sea and Prosperous Voyage*, created like *A Midsummer Night's Dream* in Berlin, was first performed at the Mendelssohn home in September 1828; *The Hebrides*, of course, originated during the composer's Scottish sojourn in August 1829.

By his twentieth year, Mendelssohn thus had either discovered the ideas or completed scores for all three overtures. His fourth published overture, *Zum Märchen von der schöne Melusine* (Op. 32), which appeared in 1836, was composed and revised in 1833–4; his fifth, the *Ouvertüre für Harmoniemusik* (Op. 24), which appeared in 1839, was a reworking of the *Notturno* for eleven wind instruments of 1824. Two other overtures, the 'Trumpet' of 1826 (revised 1833) and *Ruy Blas* of 1839, were released posthumously as Opp. 101 and 95 in 1867 and 1851.

Mendelssohn delayed considerably the process of seeing through the press *A Midsummer Night's Dream*, *Calm Sea*, and *The Hebrides*: not until 1835 were these three works issued in full score, and then as a kind of triptych, with a dedication to the Crown Prince of Prussia. Despite their disparate subject matter – a Shakespeare play, two Goethe poems, and impressions of Scotland – Mendelssohn clearly perceived in these works common compositional techniques and aesthetic approaches to what was still a relatively new genre – the programmatic concert overture. In an enthusiastic letter of 20 October 1835, Robert Schumann also sensed the unity of the three when he welcomed Mendelssohn ('Meritis') as the new director of the Gewandhaus in Leipzig: ' "Which of Meritis' overtures do you like the best?" asked a simpleton near me – whereupon, embracing, the keys of E minor, B minor, and D major formed a triad of the Graces, and I could think of no better answer than the best one – "Every one of them".'[3]

Mendelssohn was not the first to create independent concert overtures, but he was arguably the first major composer to probe extensively the ability of the autonomous overture to treat in purely musical terms programmatic ideas, whether of a dramatic, poetic, or pictorial nature. Of course, Beethoven had composed numerous overtures, but in some way these were associated with the stage (e.g., *Coriolanus*, *Egmont*, *Ruins of Athens*, *König Stephan*, the *Leonore* Overtures) or commissioned for a particular function (e.g., *Namensfeier*, *Die Weihe des Hauses*). Of Carl Maria von Weber's three concert overtures, at least two (*Grande ouverture à plusieurs instruments* of 1807 and *Der Beherrscher der Geister* of 1811) were reworkings of overtures to operas; the occasion for the third (the *Jubel-Ouvertüre* of 1818, which may have influenced *A Midsummer Night's Dream*; see Exx. 3–4, pp. 13–14), was a celebration of the Saxon king, Friedrich August I. Concert performances of untitled overtures or overtures borrowed from operas were commonplace in the early nineteenth century, and in the rich musical life of Berlin Mendelssohn would have heard abundant examples from Mozart, Gluck, Beethoven, Weber, Spontini, and Spohr, among many others.

Of Mendelssohn's contemporaries who produced concert overtures, Hector Berlioz, who heard Mendelssohn perform an early version of *The Hebrides* at the piano in Rome in 1831, stands out: Berlioz's *Waverley* Overture, inspired by the novels of Sir Walter Scott (albeit in a general way), was completed in 1828, the year of *Calm Sea and Prosperous Voyage*. But Berlioz and Mendelssohn came to hold sharply different views about the use of extra-musical ideas in orchestral music. While Berlioz continued to shape and reshape the programmatic details of the *Symphonie fantastique*, distributing the initial programme to the audience at the symphony's 1830 première, Mendelssohn remained characteristically reluctant to describe or discuss extra-musical ideas in his works.[4] Rather, as he emphasized in a celebrated letter of 15 October 1842 to Marc André Souchay, Mendelssohn preferred to view music as a language and syntax of sounds superior to that of words.[5] The concert overture was the genre in which he first formulated and tested extensively his solution to the problem of music as an autonomous versus a referential art. What he essentially accomplished was to separate further the overture from its traditional role on the stage, and to free orchestral music from the conventions of the symphony – in short, to secure for instrumental music unexplored avenues of romantic expression, at once 'fascinating, original, and perfectly new'. To place this accomplishment in context, we may briefly review Mendelssohn's early career in Berlin.

Since his first public appearance at age nine in a Berlin concert,[6] Mendelssohn had gained increasing recognition as a Mozart-like prodigy. The grandson of the distinguished Enlightenment philosopher Moses Mendelssohn, and son of the banker Abraham Mendelssohn, young Felix was afforded a superb education by private tutors. By the age of eleven he was reading Latin and Greek and studying mathematics and geography; lessons in drawing and painting, violin, and organ probably began as well at this time.[7] Mendelssohn's first piano teacher was his mother Lea; in 1816, during a family trip to Paris, he may have had some lessons with Marie Bigot, who had known Beethoven in Vienna; and in 1821, during a visit to Weimar to meet Goethe, Mendelssohn played for Johann Nepomuk Hummel. In Berlin, Mendelssohn's development as a pianist was entrusted to Ludwig Berger, a pupil of Muzio Clementi; in 1824, Mendelssohn received some 'finishing lessons' from Ignaz Moscheles, who promptly declared that he had encountered a master, not a pupil.[8]

Mendelssohn's rapid development as a composer was nothing short of astonishing. His earliest surviving effort was an unassuming song, written at ten, for his father's birthday on 11 December 1819. By this time, however, the boy had already begun a systematic course in figured bass, chorale, fugue, and canon with Carl Friedrich Zelter, the director of the Berlin Singakademie and confidant of Goethe. Zelter's method of instruction was largely based on Johann Philipp Kirnberger's *Die Kunst des reinen Satzes* (Berlin, 1771), a treatise intended to exemplify the teachings of J. S. Bach.[9] In Zelter's instruction are found the roots of Mendelssohn's lifelong study

3

of Bach's music and counterpoint, a fascination he later acknowledged to Johann Christian Lobe.[10]

By Mendelssohn's fifteenth birthday (3 February 1824), Zelter could declare the pupil had finished his apprenticeship and was now an independent member of the brotherhood of Mozart, Haydn, and Bach.[11] In the space of less than five years Mendelssohn had produced *sinfonie*, concertos, chamber, piano and organ works; songs; sacred works for chorus; and several short German stage works. The decidedly academic bent of his training was revealed in a proliferation of compositions in the severe style, most notably the series of thirteen string *sinfonie* composed between 1821 and 1823, replete with chromatic writing and fugues reminiscent of Bach, but also containing, in the finale of *Sinfonia VIII*, an impressive amalgam of fugue and sonata form modelled on the finale of Mozart's 'Jupiter' Symphony.[12] Despite this proclivity for traditional counterpoint (a reviewer in 1828 noted that 'it is as though the composer desired to announce officially just how diligently he has studied and gained complete mastery of his material through counterpoint'[13]), Mendelssohn clearly made efforts to assimilate the stylistic influence of more modern composers as well. Thus his A minor Piano Concerto (1822) is indebted to Hummel's concerto in the same key, and his two double piano concertos in E and Ab (1823 and 1824) show signs of John Field, J. L. Dussek, and Beethoven. In particular, Beethoven loomed large as a stylistic influence: in Mendelssohn's Octet, the recall of the scherzo in the finale – a device borrowed from Beethoven's Fifth Symphony – is but one clear example.[14]

In 1825 Abraham sought the advice of Luigi Cherubini in Paris about his son's prospects as a composer. In the youth's portfolio were at least two works that showed the range of his compositional interests: a Kyrie in D minor for five-part chorus and orchestra, written in a learned contrapuntal style recalling Mozart's Requiem, and his fourth piano quartet, Op. 3 in B minor, which included among its four movements an extended Beethovenian first movement in modified sonata form and a sprightly Mendelssohnian scherzo for its third. Cherubini's verdict – 'ce garçon est riche; il fera bien' – reinforced Mendelssohn's choice of profession. On their return from Paris, the Mendelssohns stopped in Weimar where Felix presented Goethe with a copy of the piano quartet; by June they had reached Berlin, and just four months later Felix completed the work that marked a startling new order of excellence: the Octet, his first masterpiece.

In this context of his precocity and accelerating maturation, Mendelssohn's path to the programmatic concert overture, which reached its first substantial goal in *A Midsummer Night's Dream* of August 1826, should be examined. Two works, the Octet and 'Trumpet' Overture (October 1825–March 1826), provide some crucial, though generally disregarded, evidence about his approach to programmaticism, form, and orchestration in *A Midsummer Night's Dream*. The critical movement from the Octet is the third, the elfin scherzo in G minor; in its transparent, delicate textures is a prototype for the string music of the fairies in the overture. According to Mendelssohn's sister Fanny, the remarkable close of the scherzo, in which a lightly punctuated unison passage appears to evaporate into thin air, was prompted by a passage from Goethe's *Faust*:

The ethereal, fanciful, and spirit-like scherzo in this [Octet] is something quite new. He tried to set to music the stanza from the Walpurgis-night Dream in 'Faust': – 'The flight of the clouds and the veil of mist/Are lighted from above./A breeze in the leaves, a wind in the reeds,/And all has vanished.' 'And he has been really successful,' says Fanny of this Ottetto, in her biography of Felix. 'To me alone he told his idea: the whole piece is to be played staccato and pianissimo, the tremulandos [*sic*] coming in now and then, the trills passing away with the quickness of lightning; everything new and strange, and at the same time most insinuating and pleasing, one feels so near the world of spirits, carried away in the air, half inclined to snatch up a broomstick and follow the aerial procession. At the end the first violin takes a flight with a feather-like lightness, and – all has vanished.'[15]

The 'Walpurgis-night Dream' to which Fanny referred was the extraordinary dream-like sequence in the first part of Goethe's epic directly after the 'Walpurgis-night' scene. Just as Goethe's 'Traum' is labelled an intermezzo, so does Mendelssohn's scherzo, intermezzolike, serve as a capricious interruption between the more serious slow movement and the weighty, *tour de force* contrapuntal finale of the Octet. But Goethe's 'Traum' invites further consideration. First of all, sprinkled throughout the passage are references to a Kapellmeister, who beseeches the diminutive members of his orchestra, 'Snout of Fly, Mosquito Nose,/Damnable amateurs!/Frog O'Leaves and Crick't O'Grass/You are musicians, sirs!'[16] And the final lines of the dream, the quatrain that inspired the close of Mendelssohn's scherzo, are assigned by Goethe to the 'Orchester (*Pianissimo*)'. Still more significant are the full title of Goethe's scene, 'Walpurgisnachtstraum oder Oberons und Titanias goldne Hochzeit' ('Walpurgisnight's Dream, or the Golden Wedding of Oberon and Titania'), and intermittent appearances throughout the scene by Oberon, Titania, and Puck. In introducing these three figures Goethe was alluding not to Shakespeare's play, but to C. M. Wieland's verse epic poem *Oberon* (1780), the *romantisches Heldengedicht* (based in turn on a thirteenth-century *chanson de geste*) that later served as a primary source for Carl Maria von Weber's opera *Oberon* (1826). Nevertheless, for the impressionable young Mendelssohn beginning to read the Schlegel-Tieck translations of Shakespeare, the leap from Goethe's epic to Shakespeare's play, from the fanciful 'Walpurgisnachtstraum' to an orchestral work (*pianissimo*) on the 'Sommernachtstraum', must not have been difficult. Mendelssohn would have discovered related imagery for such a composition in Goethe's verses and in the scherzo of his own Octet.

In a similar way the 'Trumpet' Overture bears critically on *A Midsummer Night's Dream*. Completed on 4 March 1826, only five months before its companion, the 'Trumpet' Overture served as a preliminary opportunity for Mendelssohn to explore certain issues of formal structure and orchestration. Though he left no clues about the programmatic content, if any, of the overture, the work exhibits some features in form, tonal structure, and orchestration that tie it to the three overtures considered in this volume. In particular, we may identify the motto-like use of a recurring fanfare, the application of mediant relationships, and the exploration of the colouristic potential of the orchestra.

The 'Trumpet' Overture begins with a brass fanfare that returns (reharmonized) near the end of the development section, reenters (again reharmonized) at the beginning of the recapitulation, and appears (in abbreviated form) at the very end of the composition. As Eduard Devrient pointed out, Mendelssohn reused its elongated rhythmic configuration (♪ | ♩ ♩ | ♩↷♩↷♩) in a more concise version in *The Hebrides* Overture, where it emerges at the end of the exposition and then figures in the development and coda (𝄾 ↱ ♫ ♩ ♩ | ♩↷♩↷○ |).[17] The four-fold statement of the fanfare in the 'Trumpet' Overture anticipates the three-fold, motto-like presentation of the opening wind chords in *A Midsummer Night's Dream*, which return to mark the recapitulation and the end of that overture. In both works a wind motive serves as a defining gesture that recurs to underscore the organic unity of the musical structure.

In the 'Trumpet' Overture the fanfare melodically defines the third C to E, and is initially accompanied by the tonic C major and the submediant A major, the third below. Near the conclusion of the development Mendelssohn touches upon E major, the mediant above the tonic; and much of the development is devoted to juxtapositions of third-related keys. In *A Midsummer Night's Dream*, a third relation is embedded in the motto of the very opening: the ambivalent pitches of the first chord, E–G♯, may be heard as part of an E major (tonic) or C♯ minor (submediant) harmony, and indeed C♯ minor later emerges as the goal of the development section.

This extensive use of mediant relationships acts to weaken the traditional hegemony of the tonic–dominant axis in favour of colourful relationships of more remotely related keys. Of course, Mendelssohn was not the originator of this device; the late works of Mozart and Haydn offer mediant progressions, and Beethoven developed the technique further (e.g., first movements of the Op. 31 no. 1, 'Waldstein', and 'Hammerklavier' Piano Sonatas), as did Schubert (first movement of the 'Great' Symphony in C major, D 944, which Mendelssohn would perform in Leipzig in 1839). But Mendelssohn may have been the first to ally the use of mediant relationships with a special type of orchestration, based on nuance and understatement, that he first tested in the development of the 'Trumpet' Overture and then reused in that of *The Hebrides*. In this device Mendelssohn contraposed wind figures, drawn from the related mottoes and placed in clearly articulated, shifting groups of instruments, against subdued harmonic backdrops in the strings (Ex. 1), effectively creating a kaleidoscope of changing wind colours against a soft, undulating wash of string sound. Similar scoring procedures obtain in the developments of *A Midsummer Night's Dream* and *Calm Sea and Prosperous Voyage*, though in these works the device is not necessarily restricted to individual mediant relationships. Especially masterful is the orchestration in the development of *A Midsummer Night's Dream*, where the orchestral palette is expanded by including touches of *pianissimo* brass with individual colours of the woodwind group.

In many ways the 'Trumpet' Overture could be viewed as a preliminary study for *A Midsummer Night's Dream*, though the special relationship between these works is usually overlooked in the literature, apparently because of the absence of programmatic elements in the 'Trumpet' Overture. But the scherzo of the Octet, an exemplar of that type of capricious scherzo for which Mendelssohn became so celebrated, and surely an adumbration of the special string writing in *A Midsummer Night's Dream*, does suggest that his most original work from the 1820s was concerned with programmatic ideas. The extent to which the evanescent textures of *A Midsummer Night's Dream* were at the centre of his stylistic development at this critical time may be seen in the contemporaneous *Charakterstück* in E major for piano, Op. 7 no. 7, which appeared in 1827. This miniature sonata-form movement, marked *sempre staccato e pianissimo*, appears as a kind of study whose content and mood have essentially been transferred to the keyboard from *A Midsummer Night's Dream* Overture (Ex. 2). In the first edition

Ex. 1a 'Trumpet' Overture Op. 101, beginning of development

this piece appeared with the title 'Leicht und luftig' ('Light and airy'), a title that brings to mind the closing quatrain from Goethe's 'Walpurgisnachtstraum', which had inspired the scherzo of the Octet. In a similar way the words of Hermann Franck, a friend of Mendelssohn who reviewed the *Charakterstück*, return us to the sound-world of the Octet:

All flies past hastily, without rest, gathering together in colourful throngs, and then scattering in a puff. So this splendid piece impresses as a fleet-footed daughter of the air. Individual chords seem to sting before they resolve; again and again one is teased, as if in a foggy dream. All seems to resolve in a mild, limpid twilight, an indescribably lovely effect.[18]

8

Ex. 1b *The Hebrides* Overture, beginning of development

Franck further described the character of the music as 'strange' ('fremd-artige'), recalling Fanny's description of the Octet, 'everything new and strange', which, in turn, anticipated Shaw's 1892 assessment of *A Midsummer Night's Dream* as 'fascinating, original, and perfectly new'. If the Octet and *Charakterstück* remained generically separated examples in the strange

Ex. 2 *Charakterstück* Op. 7 no. 7 ('Leicht und luftig'), beginning

9

stylistic world Mendelssohn explored during the late 1820s, the concert overture came to inspire again and again his most experimental music, and enabled him, indeed, to discover his own identity as a composer.

Genesis

The first document to come down to us about the three overtures is a
letter of 7 July 1826; here Mendelssohn reported to his sister Fanny his
intent 'to dream the *Midsummer Night's Dream*', that is, to begin the overture,
an enterprise he likened to a 'grenzenlose Kühnheit' ('a boundless boldness').[1] Not until April 1835, however, did the overture and its two companions appear in full score from Breitkopf & Härtel. This nine-year period
of conception, gestation, composition, revision and performance (in varying
orders), and publication spanned the end of Mendelssohn's student period
in Berlin; his years of travel in England and Scotland, Italy, Switzerland,
and France; his first appointment as music director in Düsseldorf; and his
arrival in Leipzig to assume the position at the Gewandhaus as municipal
music director. During this extended period, Mendelssohn came to view
the three overtures, conceived and composed separately, as a related group
of compositions that should be published together in full score, ideally
with the same opus number. The complex chronologies of the overtures,
which describe three quite intricate paths, have never been examined in
detail; and so our first task must be to reconstruct their course, thereby to
understand more fully Mendelssohn's own views of the overtures, and,
indeed, to determine how the three compositions were created.

A Midsummer Night's Dream (1826–35)

Between 1797 and 1810 August Wilhelm Schlegel issued his widely acclaimed
translations of Shakespeare's plays, including *Ein Sommernachtstraum*.[2] In
1825 a reissue of Schlegel's translations began to appear, and in all like-
lihood Mendelssohn first came to know the play well around this time. In
Schlegel's German version he would have found ample inspiration for the
overture, as in Theseus' lines in the forest, Act IV, Scene 1: 'We will, fair
Queen, up to the mountain's top,/ And mark the musical confusion [in
Schlegel's version, 'melodische Verwirrung' ('melodic confusion')]/ Of

hounds and echo in conjunction', and Hippolyta's response, 'I never heard/ So musical a discord ['so harmon'schen Zwist der Töne' ('such a harmonic discord of tones')], such sweet thunder'.

Schlegel had translated only seventeen plays, and in 1830 Ludwig Tieck began to expand the project by releasing translations of others. By 1833 the new, collaborative Schlegel–Tieck edition was completed.[3] But Tieck's contribution did not end there. Summoned to Berlin in 1841 by Friedrich Wilhelm IV to revitalize the theatre, Tieck directed the 1843 production of *A Midsummer Night's Dream* for which Mendelssohn, also brought to Berlin by the king, was commissioned to compose the famous incidental music (published in 1844 as Mendelssohn's Op. 61).[4]

In 1825 the Mendelssohn family had moved to a spacious new residence in Berlin at No. 3 Leipzigerstrasse. According to the account of Sebastian Hensel, in the garden house of the property, during the summer months of 1826, the Mendelssohn children 'led a fantastic, dreamlike life. . . . the summer months were like one uninterrupted festival day, full of poetry, music, merry games, ingenious practical jokes, disguises, and representations'.[5] During this time the children maintained a journal, with fanciful contributions from adults and children alike; in his letter of 7 July 1826, the adolescent Mendelssohn referred to 'Gartenunfug' ('garden mischief') and games that were played on the surrounding lawns. In the garden he composed piano pieces, and, evidently, began work on the overture.

We owe to Adolf Bernhard Marx (1795?–1866), a pupil of Zelter, editor of the *Berliner allgemeine musikalische Zeitung* (1824–30) and from 1830 a music professor at the University of Berlin, an especially detailed account of the overture's creation, evidence that merits citation in full:

I can still see him entering my room with a heated expression, pacing up and down a few times, and saying: 'I have a terrific idea! What do you think of it? I want to write an overture to *A Midsummer Night's Dream*.' I expressed warm support for the idea. A few days later he, the happy, free one, was back again with the score, complete up to the second part. The dance of the elves with its introductory chords was as one would later know it. Then – well, then there followed an overture, cheerful, pleasantly agitated, perfectly delightful, perfectly praiseworthy – only I could perceive no *Midsummer Night's Dream* in it. Sincerely feeling that it was my duty as a friend, I told him this in candor. He was taken aback, irritated, even hurt, and ran out without taking his leave. I let that pass and avoided his house for several days, for since my last visit, following that exchange, his mother and Fanny had also received me coldly, with something approaching hostility.

A few days later, the Mendelssohns' slim manservant appeared at my door and handed me an envelope with the words 'A compliment from Mr. Felix'. When I opened it great pieces of torn-up manuscript paper fell to the ground, along with a note from Felix reading: 'You are always right! But now come and help'. Perhaps the very understanding, thoughtful father had made the difference; or perhaps the hotheaded young man had come to himself.

I did not fail to respond; I hurried over and explained that, as I saw it, such a score, since it serves as a prologue, must give a true and complete reflection of the drama. He went to work with fire and absolute dedication. At least the wanderings of the young pairs of lovers could be salvaged from the first draft, in the first motive (E, D♯ D♮, C♯); everything else was created anew. It was pointless to resist! 'It's too full! too much!' he cried, when I wanted him to make room for the ruffians and even for Bottom's ardent ass's braying. It was done; the overture became the one we now know. Mother and sister were reconciled when they saw the composer rushing around in high excitement and pleasure. But during the first performance at his house, the father declared in front of the numerous assembly that it was actually more my work than Felix's. This was naturally quite unjustified, whether it was merely to express his gratification at my behavior, or perhaps to give me satisfaction for the earlier defection of the womenfolk. The original idea and the execution belonged to Felix, the advice I had given was my duty and my only part in it.[6]

Though no doubt biased,[7] Marx's claims for influencing the course of the overture's creation are partially supported by an undated, incomplete, autograph orchestral score in the M. Deneke Mendelssohn Collection of the Bodleian Library, Oxford.[8] Containing 127 bars, the fragment begins with the familiar four wind chords and the scurrying E minor fairies' music for strings, almost exactly as we know these passages. But at the first *forte* tutti, marking the bridge to the dominant and second thematic group, the manuscript diverges from the final version. To be sure, the tutti passage is 'cheerful, pleasantly agitated, perfectly delightful, perfectly praiseworthy'. As Ex. 3 reveals, it begins by outlining an ascending arpeggiation, G♯–B–E–G♯, a clear reference to the ascending motion of the opening

Ex. 3 *A Midsummer Night's Dream* Overture Op. 21, bridge, first version (Oxford, Bodleian Library, M. Deneke Mendelssohn Collection, b. 5)

Example 4 C. M. von Weber, *Jubel* Overture

wind chords. The passage then asserts the descending tetrachord E–D♯–
C♯–B, clearly a metamorphosis of the minor tetrachord, E–D♮–C♮–B, so
prominent in the fairies' music. Mendelssohn thus took care to derive the
forte passage directly from the opening bars of the work. On the other hand,
the passage is marred by square phrasing and considerable repetition, possibly revealing the haste with which it was composed. Furthermore, the
beginning of the passage seems to contain a thinly veiled allusion to Carl
Maria von Weber's *Jubel* Overture (Ex. 4), an appropriate reminiscence, perhaps, given the celebratory tone of Weber's overture and the 'regal', programmatic elements shared by the two. Weber's overture was first performed
on 20 September 1818, to celebrate the fiftieth anniversary of the reign of the
Saxon king Friedrich August I.[9] Mendelssohn's passage (and its revised
form in the final version of the overture) invokes the court of Theseus,
Duke of Athens. Perhaps for Marx (and for Mendelssohn) the familiarity
of the Weber overture worked to vitiate the special, strange quality required
by *A Midsummer Night's Dream*, and so the passage was ultimately scrapped
and recast.

Further on in the Bodleian fragment, at the turn to the dominant, the
manuscript again transmits the overture as we know it, that is, bars 97ff of
the final version, leading up to the second thematic complex. But before the
second group emerges, the draft breaks off. Now according to Marx's
account, Mendelssohn in fact did complete the second theme, intended to
represent the 'wanderings of the young pairs of lovers'. Perhaps this theme,
and the subsequent conclusion of the exposition, was the portion of the
early draft that was delivered to Marx in torn pieces.

The Oxford fragment permits three additional observations about the
original shape of the overture. First, Mendelssohn titled the work simply
Ouvertüre, without an explicit reference to the play. Second, the original
tempo marking was Molto Allegro e vivace, instead of the Allegro di molto

of the final version. Third, and most significantly, the original draft did not include a part for the ophicleide, the instrument used with great effect in the final version to portray the boorish Bottom the Weaver. The absence of the ophicleide in the Oxford draft might bear out Marx's claim that he persuaded Mendelssohn to 'make room for the ruffians and even for Bottom's ardent ass's braying' – in short, to expand the exposition in order to include musical motives for all the groups of characters in the play.

In any event, Mendelssohn worked quickly to revise and finish the overture; a second, completed autograph full score, now in the Biblioteca Jagiellońska, Kraków, bears the date 6 August 1826.[10] This little-known source establishes that the overture was composed in about one month, between 6 July and 6 August 1826. The layout of the Kraków manuscript is nearly identical to that of the Bodleian draft. However, Mendelssohn now indicated the subject of his overture, though parenthetically, by inscribing the heading 'Ouvertüre (zum Sommernachtstraum)'. What is more, he re-arranged the staves to accommodate a part for an English bass horn ('Corno inglese di basso'), a 'variety of upright serpent in the shape of a bassoon'.[11] He employed the bass horn in two other works – the *Notturno* for eleven Winds (1824),[12] subsequently rescored and released in 1839 as the Overture for wind instruments, Op. 24, and the *Trauermarsch* for Norbert Burgmüller (1836), published posthumously as Op. 103 (1868) – in which the instrument generally plays with a contrabassoon. By the mid 1830s, the bass horn was increasingly being replaced by the ophicleide, a member of the keyed bugle family.[13] Thus, when Mendelssohn published the score of *A Midsummer Night's Dream* in 1835, he indicated the ophicleide. But the original inspiration for this part was the 'pretty, deep sound' of the English bass horn, an addition that may have been influenced by Marx's counsel.

The Kraków autograph is a relatively clean copy, with only occasional, fastidiously notated changes in orchestration and voice leading; it essentially presents the overture as we now know it. The manuscript does contain, however, one large-scale excision, a passage of thirty-four bars that originally appeared in the closing section of the exposition between bars 229 and 230 (Ex. 5). Characterized by a repetitive emphasis of the dominant, the passage was wisely rejected by Mendelssohn.

According to accounts by Marx, Eduard Devrient, and W. A. Lampadius,[14] the overture was first performed with full orchestra in the Mendelssohn home, presumably sometime in 1826 after 6 August. In addition, Mendelssohn and his sister Fanny presented it as a piano duet for Ignaz Moscheles in Berlin on 19 November 1826.[15] The first public

b.230 follows

Ex. 5 *A Midsummer Night's Dream* Overture Op. 21 (Kraków, Biblioteca
Jagiellońska, Mendelssohn Nachlass 32)

performance for full orchestra took place in Stettin on 20 February 1827,
in a concert directed by Karl Loewe. A review published in the *Berliner
allgemeine musikalische Zeitung* compared the fairies' music, with its
scoring for divided strings, to 'swarms of insects that aroused a pleasant,
lively tumult in the setting rays of the sun', and mentioned the comical
usage of the bass horn, which 'entered into the subject, wonderfully
enough, like a great pair of ass's ears in fine company'.[16]

Later in 1827 Mendelssohn matriculated at the University of Berlin
and, according to Ferdinand Hiller, worked intensely on the overture,

extemporizing on its themes at the piano between attending lectures at the university (the Kraków manuscript, however, establishes that the overture was in virtually final form by August 1826). Hiller himself first heard the work rendered by Mendelssohn at the piano in Frankfurt am Main in September 1827.[17] Owing to the efforts of Mendelssohn's friend Friedrich Lindblad, the overture was performed in Sweden in 1828, but it received a mixed reception, largely as the result of the Swedish audience's lack of familiarity with the play.[18]

Two performances introduced the work to England in 1829: in the Argyle Rooms in London, on 24 June (Midsummer Night) at a concert of the flautist Louis François Philippe Drouet, where the work was encored, and there again on 13 July, in a benefit concert organized by Mendelssohn for the relief of victims from flooding in Silesia.[19] A reviewer in the *Harmonicon* noted that the overture was 'sparkling with genius and rich in effect; some parts playful and sylph-like, others lofty and solid; the whole indicating that the musician has studied the poet, has entered into his thoughts, and even caught some of his imagination'.[20] A third English performance, conducted by Sir George Smart, followed on 1 March 1830 at the Philharmonic Society of London.[21]

By this time, Mendelssohn was preparing to embark on his journey to Switzerland, Italy, and France. Two years later, on 19 February 1832, the overture was performed in Paris by F.-A. Habeneck at the Société des Concerts du Conservatoire, after it had received four careful rehearsals, in one of which Mendelssohn himself played the timpani part. According to brief accounts by the composer and Hiller,[22] the performance was a success; to Hiller we owe this amusing anecdote:

For the performance a place had been given [Mendelssohn] in a box on the grand tier, with a couple of distinguished musical amateurs. During the last *forte*, after which the fairies return once more, one of these gentlemen said to the other: 'C'est très-bien, très-bien, mais nous savons le reste;' and they slipped out without hearing the 'reste' [i.e., the unexpected *piano* metamorphosis in bs 663ff. of the regal music from bs 62ff., and the equally unexpected return of the wind chords at the close], and without any idea that they had been sitting next [to] the composer.

Curiously, these accounts were later contradicted by Franz Liszt, who, writing in 1858, asserted that the overture had not even been performed: 'The Overture to *A Midsummer Night's Dream* was a fiasco at the Conservatory in Paris some twenty-five years ago (I was there); before the living Mendelssohn not one single note of his composition was played.'[23] Probably in retrospect Liszt confused the overture with the *Reformation*

Symphony, which, though rehearsed by Habeneck, was not performed.[24] The overture was indeed performed, for it received this withering rebuke from F.-J. Fétis in the *Revue musicale*:

I should say that this work does not seem to me to justify the praise given it by the author's friends. Its forms are not ordinary, but I find in it more an affectation of originality than a genuine originality. I certainly concede its express intent to depart from those habits of musical conduct and modulation in which, it is true, we are a bit routine, but the fantasy of the work seems like something that has been arranged in cold blood; it is monotonous and lacks life. The first motive appears to promise something, but the effect soon vanishes. I do not speak of incorrect harmonies and of the scorn for the art of writing which generally appears in this composition. Monsieur Mendelssohn is from a school where one is not very severe about these sorts of things.[25]

In 1829 Mendelssohn had met the redoubtable Belgian critic in London and had become embroiled in a controversy about Purcell (whose 'incorrect harmonies' Fétis claimed Mendelssohn had disparaged), Croft, and other English composers. Mendelssohn had attempted to clear his name by writing a rebuttal to Fétis in the form of an 'English letter' to the *Harmonicon*.[26] Now, in 1832, Fétis evidently attempted to retaliate by attacking Mendelssohn's overture, as we read in this unpublished passage from the composer's letter of 28 February 1832 to his parents in Berlin: '*à propos* humour and overture, Fétis has raked me over horribly in his journal, and said I cannot write cleanly and cannot orchestrate, and I have a usurped reputation. Alas! He has always cut the most dreadful faces before me here, and never greeted me. The English letter is still under his skin, and so he won't have anything to do with me.'[27]

While in Paris Mendelssohn took the decision to publish the overture in parts and piano-duet arrangement. On 19 April 1832 he sent the parts to Breitkopf & Härtel; then, on 5 July, after his arrival in England, a rehearsal of the duet arrangement with Moscheles on 5 June, and a successful performance of the overture at a Philharmonic concert on 18 June, he sent the duet arrangement to Breitkopf & Härtel.[28] On 10 July, the parts and arrangement were published in England by Cramer, Addison & Beale; Mendelssohn's autograph of the arrangement, evidently prepared for the English publication, bears the title 'Overture/ to/ Shakespeare's Midsummer-nightsdream [*sic*]/ arranged/ as a Duet for two performers/ by/ Felix Mendelssohn Bartholdy'.[29] Not until December 1832 and March 1833 did the parts and arrangement appear in Germany.[30] On 27 March Gottfried Fink, the editor of the Leipzig *Allgemeine musikalische Zeitung*, published a lengthy, fanciful

interpretation of the overture, translated in the *Harmonicon* with this somewhat puckish comment by the English editor:

The beauty of M. Mendelssohn's overture has excited in M. Fink's mind a lively
recollection of Shakspeare's [*sic*] most fanciful drama, and almost turned the brain
of the critic. He has wrought himself into a belief that music is equal to language
in the power of describing. His reverie is amusing; but the intimate acquaintance he
manifests with the works of our great dramatic poet is a circumstance more gratifying
to us than all the sallies of his imagination.[31]

Having returned to Berlin in the summer of 1832, Mendelssohn made preparations for several German performances of the overture. In Berlin it was
heard publicly on 15 November, along with the first and only performance
during his lifetime of the *Reformation* Symphony, Op. 107; the overture
impressed Ludwig Rellstab as 'a fantastic, intellectual work that allows
Shakespeare's romantic play to shimmer through in a happy tone painting'.[32]
Subsequently the overture was used to open two Berlin concerts, in
December 1832 and February 1833.[33] Meanwhile, in Leipzig Breitkopf &
Härtel arranged for a performance on 21 February conducted by Christian
August Pohlenz, Mendelssohn's predecessor at the Gewandhaus,[34] and for
this occasion asked Mendelssohn to supply a programmatic sketch of the
overture. The composer's answer, contained in a letter of 15 February 1833,
illustrates clearly his distrust of musical programmes: 'To reveal my train of
thought in the composition for the programme is really not possible for me,
since that train of thought is, in fact, my overture.' But then, noting that the
overture was closely related to the play, he obligingly outlined the essential
dramatic elements of the music (see p. 72 below). In addition, he requested
that the basic elements of the play be summarized on the programme.
Beyond this, however, he did not venture, explaining that 'if the overture is
well written, then it can competently speak for itself; if, on the other hand,
it is not well written, then a written explanation is certainly of no avail'.[35]

The final stage in the history of *A Midsummer Night's Dream* as an independent concert overture was Mendelssohn's decision to release it, along
with the *The Hebrides* and *Calm Sea and Prosperous Voyage*, in full score.
Writing to Breitkopf & Härtel on 29 November 1833 and 14 March 1834,
the composer expressed his wish that the three appear with the same opus
number and as 'Drei Concert-Ouvertüren', 'so that one could see that they
belong together'. In addition, he explored the possibility of commissioning
vignettes for the three title pages. By 29 July he decided to dedicate all
three scores to the Crown Prince of Prussia, even though the piano-duet
arrangement of *The Hebrides* had already appeared with a dedication to the

singer Franz Hauser. And he reiterated his desire that the opus number 27 be assigned for all three works (in fact, opus 27 was eventually retained by Breitkopf & Härtel for *Calm Sea and Prosperous Voyage*, the final overture to go through the press; numbers 21 and 26 had already been assigned to the earlier publications of *A Midsummer Night's Dream* and *The Hebrides*). Finally, he again reaffirmed his notion that all three scores should appear simultaneously as one work.[36] The three overtures were published without opus number around May 1835 with the title, *Drei Concert-Ouverturen. No. 1. Der Sommernachtstraum. No. 2. Die Fingals-Höhle. No. 3. Meeresstille und glückliche Fahrt.* An enthusiastic review in the *Allgemeine musikalische Zeitung*, the house organ of Breitkopf & Härtel, greeted the three works as among Mendelssohn's most significant, and among the most important overtures produced up to that time.[37]

Calm Sea and Prosperous Voyage (1828–35)

In 1822 Beethoven's cantata *Meeresstille und glückliche Fahrt*, Op. 112, appeared in full score with a dedication to Goethe; on 17 November 1824 A. B. Marx devoted a lengthy review to the work in his new journal, the *Berliner allgemeine musikalische Zeitung*.[38] Just at this time the young Mendelssohn was struggling to come to terms with Beethoven's music. The C minor Symphony, Op. 11 (first performed on Fanny's birthday, 14 November 1824), with its triumphant conclusion in C major, is one example in a series of increasingly Beethovenian works that would include the Piano Sonatas, Opp. 6 and 106 (1826 and 1827), the String Quartet in A minor, Op. 13 (1827), and the *Calm Sea and Prosperous Voyage* Overture (1828).[39] For Marx, Beethoven had compellingly 'rehumanized' instrumental music by basing symphonies on fundamentally extra-musical ideas (*Grundideen*), subjective ideas that in the Fifth Symphony had developed into 'a series of psychological states represented with great psychological accuracy'.[40] As Judith Silber Ballan has argued, Marx's theories about musical aesthetics, and his review of Beethoven's texted cantata may well have encouraged Mendelssohn to attempt an independent concert overture on the same subject.[41]

The first mention of the overture occurs in a letter Mendelssohn wrote to Karl Klingemann on 5 February 1828:[42] 'For myself, I wish to be vindicated by a grand Overture to Goethe's *Meeresstille und glückliche Fahrt*. I have the work already in mind – the thick waves will be represented by the contrabassoon.' By 22 April the 'Ouvertüre *à grand* Orchester' had been planned in detail,[43] and by May had been drafted. Early in May Marx brought out his treatise *Über Malerei in der Tonkunst (On Painting in Music)*, where he developed most cogently his thesis that instrumental music was developing inexorably toward programmaticism. Marx observed that Beethoven, in his cantata on *Meeresstille*, had not dared to dispense with Goethe's words; rather, this task was left to one of Beethoven's 'students', 'Felix Mendelssohn Bartholdy, who has realized this idea, to express *Meeresstille und glückliche Fahrt* without words'.[44]

Writing to Klingemann on 18 June, Fanny divulged that her brother was still preoccupied with the overture and that, in deference to the bipartite structure of Goethe's poem, he had envisaged the overture as two 'tableaux',[45] lest the first part, the Adagio representing *Calm Sea*, be misconstrued as a slow introduction. (Indeed, in the score Mendelssohn carefully avoids a strong cadence at the end of the Adagio by eliding it with the ensuing Allegro.) According to Devrient, the overture was performed at Mendelssohn's home during the summer of 1828; a more specific date for the performance, 8 September 1828, is reported in the memoirs of Johann Gustav Droysen.[46]

Two of Mendelssohn's first acts after he arrived in England in April 1829 were to perform the overture at the keyboard for Klingemann and to consider having it presented at the Philharmonic concerts.[47] Returning to Berlin, where he contracted measles, Mendelssohn dictated a letter to Lindblad on 11 April 1830. In this little-known document the composer explained that he had intended to send his Swedish friend a copy of the overture, but that the copy, along with the original manuscript, had been stolen. In lieu of the copy, Mendelssohn offered this description of the work:

The introduction (*Meeresstille*) I have planned this way, that a pitch gently sustained by the strings for a long while hovers here and there and trembles, barely audible, so that in the slowest Adagio now the basses, now the violins, rest on the same pitch for several bars. The whole stirs sluggishly from the passage with heavy tedium. Finally it comes to a halt with thick chords, and then the *glückliche Fahrt* sets out. Now all the wind instruments, the timpani, oboes, and flutes begin and play merrily until the end. Piccolos also enter toward the middle, and there is a murderous uproar. I think the thing will please you, for it strikes me as fresh.[48]

On the whole, Mendelssohn's sketchy account corresponds to the overture as we know it, with two exceptions. First, the published version calls for only one piccolo. A more significant alteration concerns the description of the opening. Evidently, the original version began with several static bars in which the basses and then the violins sustained the same pitch for several bars, a beginning perhaps influenced by the opening of Beethoven's cantata, which commences with two full bars of a sustained chord. In the final version of the overture, of course, the cellos are given a static pedal point for several bars, but the essential motive of the work, the descending figure D–A–G–F♯, is heard in the contrabass in the very first two bars. Considerably later in *Calm Sea* (bs 29ff), the violins are assigned the pedal point, possibly a vestige of the original conception.

In May 1830, at the beginning of his two-year period of travels, Mendelssohn visited Dessau, where, according to Julius Schubring, he allowed the overture to be rehearsed.[49] But apparently not until 1 December 1832 was the overture performed in public, at a benefit concert in Berlin. According to an anonymous reviewer, the composition represented a

tone painting (*Tongemälde*) for orchestra which offered a musical commentary on Goethe's two poems . . . according to their principal characters. Although this can be accomplished far more impressively through song (as was accomplished by Beethoven), nevertheless one must not deny that the language of music can also depict quite successfully the calm of the ocean, the swelling of the sails, etc.; to that extent the execution of this idea as grasped by Herr Felix Mendelssohn-Bartholdy was quite successful. The second part of this musical fantasia, it seemed to us, was perhaps somewhat too long, and perhaps touched here and there too closely on Beethoven.[50]

After the Berlin performance, Mendelssohn put the overture aside until November 1833, when he proposed that Breitkopf & Härtel publish his three concert overtures in full score. But writing from Düsseldorf to Devrient on 5 February 1834 Mendelssohn admitted that he still intended to revise nearly the whole of *Prosperous Voyage*.[51] We learn a good deal more about these revisions in a letter the composer penned to his mother on 19 February 1834:

In the last few weeks I have again turned to the *Calm Sea*, which is also to appear in score. I felt keenly that I have to change quite a bit – I have preferred to write an entirely new score, since the old one, in any case, was stolen, and have reworked the piece from the ground up. I think it is immeasurably better than before, and I have taken pleasure in noting while at work that I am becoming more clever. The main revision concerns the passage from the first entrance of the piccolo up to the entrance of the timpani at the end. Between these two places nothing has remained the same, except the two melodic passages for the high cello and the clarinet in its low register. The entire part of the piccolo, the arrangement and reappearance of the theme are different and less ambiguous. In the *Meeresstille* I have made only slight improvements in the instrumentation and voice leading, and up to the entrance of the piccolo I haven't changed anything, but only tied it more closely together. I would like to hear it once.[52]

In the printed version of the score the piccolo does not enter until b. 286, near the beginning of the development section in *Prosperous Voyage*. The timpani passage is undoubtedly that of bs 465ff in the coda, the passage marking the arrival of the vessel in the port. The references to the cello and clarinet passages may be identified as two statements of the second theme: one for cello in C major in the development (bs 335ff), and one for clarinet in D major at the beginning of the recapitulation (bs 379ff). In summary, the revisions Mendelssohn undertook in February 1834 evidently affected primarily the development and recapitulation of *Prosperous Voyage*.

According to Mendelssohn the original 1828 autograph of the overture, which would reveal the full extent of these revisions, was stolen in 1830. Presumably, the composer prepared a second manuscript of the 1828 version. In the M. Deneke Mendelssohn Collection in the Bodleian Libary at Oxford there are eight autograph pages in full score that transmit an early version of some 100 bars from the exposition of *Prosperous Voyage*. Though a date for this fragment cannot be established, the layout and calligraphy of the manuscript resemble that of the 1826 autographs of *A Midsummer Night's Dream*, and the attractive possibility exists that the fragment transmits a passage from the lost 1828 version.[53]

Three passages from the exposition – the bridge to the second theme, the second theme, and the closing section – are contained in the Bodleian manuscript. In this early version Mendelssohn prepared the second theme with a flowing tremolo figure in the strings on the secondary dominant (E major), not unlike the printed version (bs 175ff), where, however, the tremolo is divided between the winds and strings. But as Ex. 6a illustrates, in the Bodleian version the tremolo was meant to hover above a protracted dominant pedal point on A in the contrabass, creating a harmonically blended wash of sound. What is more, Mendelssohn arranged to have the opening bass motive of *Calm Sea* appear in the first bassoon in double augmentation, as if to strengthen the thematic coherence between *Calm Sea* and *Prosperous Voyage*.

The Oxford version of the second theme resembles closely its counterpart in the printed score: the twelve-bar theme is heard twice, first in the cellos, and then in the flutes and clarinets doubled by the cellos. But what follows differs considerably from the printed version. Instead of the compact reworking of the rhythmic figure from the second theme (bs 209ff), and the crescendo to the trumpet fanfares marking the end of the exposition (bs 243ff), Mendelssohn originally inserted a lyrical six-bar theme that was immediately repeated with the direction *ritardando* (Ex. 6b). Most striking about this theme is its similarity to the 'lovers' subject' from *A Midsummer*

Ex. 6a *Calm Sea and Prosperous Voyage* Overture, Op. 27,
early version (Oxford, Bodleian Library, M. Deneke Mendelssohn, b.5)

Ex. 6b *Calm Sea and Prosperous Voyage* Overture, Op. 27,
early version (Oxford, Bodleian Library, M. Deneke Mendelssohn, b.5)

Ex. 6c *A Midsummer Night's Dream* Overture, Op. 21

Night's Dream (Ex. 6c); both have stepwise chromatic motion (descending
in one, ascending in the other), a turn to the subdominant, and a melodic
skip by fifth followed by descending stepwise motion. Perhaps the similarities
struck him as too strong, and for this reason he rejected the passage when
he revised the overture in 1834.

The remaining pages of the Oxford fragment mark the conclusion of the exposition. This section differs considerably from the printed score, especially in its omission of the boisterous brass and timpani fanfares in the final version (bs 243ff). It begins with a condensed statement on the dominant of the first theme, with its characteristic dotted rhythm repeated and extended through a crescendo. Then, in the strings, Mendelssohn brings back the rolling, wave-like quaver passage from the beginning of *Prosperous Voyage* (bs 59ff of the printed score). In the remaining bars the passage builds up to a *fortissimo* crescendo on the dominant, and, finally, an ascending A major scale in the bass recalls a passage near the beginning of *Prosperous Voyage* (bs 89–90 of the printed score) and anticipates the massively scored D major scale near the beginning of the coda (bs 482ff of the printed score).

When, in 1834, Mendelssohn contemplated a thorough revision of his overture, he prepared a new autograph score which he sent to Breitkopf & Härtel on 14 March.[54] This autograph has survived in The Pierpont Morgan Library in New York.[55] Though undated, the manuscript reveals that it served as the publisher's *Stichvorlage*: throughout the score appear engraver's notations for the page layout, and these agree with the layout of the 1835 first edition; furthermore, on the title page the archival seal of Breitkopf & Härtel appears with the number 5544, the plate number for the first edition.

Though the Pierpont Morgan autograph transmits the final version of the overture, it bears abundant testimony to the composer's ceaseless process of revision. *Calm Sea*, for instance, exhibits several minor revisions in voice-leading and scoring, very likely the 'Kleinigkeiten' to which Mendelssohn referred in his letter of 19 February 1834. And in *Prosperous Voyage*, in the bridge of the exposition, he neatly cancelled eight redundant bars with cross-hatched pen strokes. All of these improvements enabled him to report to Klingemann in May that the overture had become a 'completely different piece' and to Schubring in August that it was 'thirty times improved'.[56]

While the overture went through the press, three successful performances were given in Leipzig on 20 April, 28 September, and 5 October 1834; the third, rehearsed and directed at the Gewandhaus by the concertmaster H. A. Matthäi, was attended by the composer.[57] On 15 November 1834 Mendelssohn returned the corrected proofs of the overture to Breitkopf & Härtel and took the opportunity to enter additional changes to the score and substantial corrections to a piano–duet arrangement that had been prepared by J. D. Baldenecker; as for a piano-solo arrangement sent by the publisher, Mendelssohn expressed grave doubts whether the thick textures of the overture could be reduced satisfactorily to one instrument.[58] By

10 April 1835 he had received exemplar copies of the score and, by 25 July, of the duet and solo-piano arrangements and the orchestral parts.[59] Then, on 4 October 1835, he included the overture on his début concert at the Gewandhaus (which he conducted with a baton, at that time a still novel practice in Leipzig). It was while reviewing the concert for the *Neue Zeitschrift für Musik* that Robert Schumann took the opportunity to dub Mendelssohn 'Meritis', noting that 'the sea lay before us stretched out, still and awesome, but from the furthest horizon there played a delicate sound here and there, as if the small waves conversed to each other in a dream'.[60]

The Hebrides (Fingal's Cave) (1829–35)

Of all Mendelssohn's overtures, none demonstrates a more complex compositional process than *The Hebrides*. From the evidence of the primary sources (listed for convenience in Table 1) we know that the overture was conceived in Scotland, during the course of Mendelssohn's walking tour with Karl Klingemann (1829); its composition was finished and immediately revised in Italy (1830); it was revised again in France and England (1832); it was first performed, revised once again, and arranged by Mendelssohn for piano duet in England (1832); and it was finally published in parts, duet arrangement, and score by Breitkopf & Härtel in Germany (1833, 1834, and 1835, respectively). No less involved is the remarkably tangled history of the autograph manuscripts, which at various times were owned or examined by several distinguished musicians, including Hector Berlioz, Ferdinand Hiller, Ignaz Moscheles, William Sterndale Bennett, Sir George Smart, and Charles Gounod, who at some time jotted down the comment concerning the bass line in bar 3 of Mendelssohn's 1830 autograph of *Die Hebriden* (no. 5), 'Je crois que le Ré a été oublié à la Contre Basse'. And, finally, no less perplexing is the curious range of titles applied to the overture, including *Die Hebriden* (*The Hebrides*), *Ouvertüre zur einsamen Insel* (*Overture to the Lonely Isle*), *The Isles of Fingal*, *Ossian in Fingalshöhle* (*Ossian in Fingal's Cave*), and *Die Fingalshöhle* (*Fingal's Cave*).

The first document concerning the work is a pen-and-ink drawing, titled 'Ein Blick auf die Hebriden', that Mendelssohn executed on 7 August 1829 (no. 1 on Table 1). The view, taken from Oban on the west coast of Scotland, shows, through the gnarled branches of a tree in the foreground, Dunollie Castle on a cliff in the middleground overlooking the Firth of Lorn and, in the distance, the indistinct outlines of Morven and the Isle of Mull.[61] On the same day, the two travellers reached Mull by steamboat,

Table 1 *Sources for* The Hebrides *Overture*

1 Pen-and-ink drawing, 'Ein Blick auf die Hebriden und Morven', 7 August 1829, Oban. Bodleian Library, Oxford, M. Deneke Mendelssohn Collection, d. 2, fol. 28

2 Sketch of the opening in short score, letter of 7 August 1829, Tobermory, Mull. New York Public Library

3 Autograph sketches for the recapitulation and coda, ca. October–November 1830, Italy. Bodleian Library, M. Deneke Mendelssohn Collection, c. 47, fol. 29

4 Manuscript copy in score, *Ouvertüre zur einsamen Insel*, 11 December 1830, Rome (?). Bodleian Library, M. Deneke Mendelssohn Collection, d. 58

5 Autograph full score, *Die Hebriden*, 16 December 1830, Rome. The Pierpont Morgan Library, New York

6 Autograph score (?), *Overture to the Isles of Fingal*, presented 6 June 1832 to the Philharmonic Society, London (?)

7 Autograph arrangement for piano duet, *Overture to the Isles of Fingal*, 19 June 1832, London. Bodleian Library, Horsley papers, b.1, fols. 1–10

8 Autograph score, *The Hebrides*, 20 June 1832, London. Present location unknown

9 First edition, arrangement for piano duet, *Overture to the Isles of Fingal* (London, Mori & Lavenu), *Ouverture aux Hébrides* (*Fingals Höhle*) (Leipzig, Breitkopf & Härtel), October 1833

10 First edition, orchestral parts, *Die Hebriden* (Leipzig, Breitkopf & Härtel), June 1834

11 First edition, score, *Die Fingals-Höhle* (Leipzig, Breitkopf & Härtel), April 1835

and that evening, from the fishing village of Tobermory, they wrote a letter to Berlin, headed 'Auf einer Hebride' ('On a Hebridean Island'). 'In order to make you realize how extraordinarily the Hebrides have affected me', Mendelssohn began, 'the following came into my mind there.'[62] There followed a sketch in piano reduction of the first twenty-one bars of the overture, with full details of scoring and dynamics, and in almost exactly the final form (no. 2; Ex. 7). Thus from the beginning Mendelssohn had in mind the three-tiered sequential opening of the basic motive in B minor, D major, and F# minor, with its extraordinary, thinly veiled progression by fifths, and orchestral colours associated with that progression: violins, oboes, and clarinets (in the final version, violins, clarinets, and oboes).[63] In b. 13

27

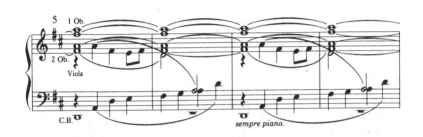

Ex. 7 *The Hebrides* Overture, Op. 26, sketch (7 August 1829)

he indicated a pause on a B major sonority and specified '*pp* tutti', 'das ganze Orchester/Paukenwirbel' ('*pp* all', 'the entire orchestra/timpani roll'); this then proceeded to an E major sonority altered to E minor before the return of the opening motive, now contraposed against the horns and trumpets. In the final version Mendelssohn opted against the pause at the B-major harmony by maintaining the undulating accompanimental figure in the lower strings (also the horns and trumpets remained silent). In the next bar he ultimately removed the turn to E major in the sketch in favour of E minor. Finally, he rebarred the work in c time instead of ¢, and compressed the rhythmic values by half.

The abundant orchestral cues of no. 2 reveal with astonishing exactitude the vividness of Mendelssohn's original concept; clearly, he intended to exploit the orchestra as a colouristic agent of his visual impressions, those recorded in the pen-and-ink drawing at Oban and those recorded mentally during the excursion to Tobermory, but – significantly – not those of Fingal's Cave, which Mendelssohn and Klingemann, of course, had not yet seen. That celebrated visit came the following morning, on 8 August. Unfortunately, we do not have Mendelssohn's impressions of the cave, for, as Klingemann explained, the composer fell victim to seasickness; Klingemann, however, left this account:

Staffa, with its strange basalt pillars and caverns, is in all the picture books. We were put out in boats and lifted by the hissing sea up the pillar stumps to the famous Fingal's Cave. A greener roar of waves never rushed into a stranger cavern – its many pillars making it look like the inside of an immense organ, black and resounding, absolutely without purpose, and quite alone, the wide grey sea within and without.[64]

The same day the travellers briefly visited the desolate island of Iona and its ruins of the monastery founded by St Columba in 563. While Klingemann found in Iona 'truly a very Ossianic and sweetly sad sound',[65] Mendelssohn again left no record of his impressions. By 9 August the two had returned to Oban, where, before they continued their journey southward to Glasgow and Liverpool, Mendelssohn found a piano on which he may have played the opening of the overture for Klingemann.[66]

Writing from Wales on 2 September and from London on 10 September, Mendelssohn referred to his overture as the 'Hebridengeschichte' ('Hebrides tale'), and on 22 September he ended a letter to his parents by quoting the opening motive in the augmented rhythmic values of his sketch of 7 August, suggesting that work on the overture had not yet advanced much beyond the initial concept. References to his visit to the Hebrides occur in letters from April 1830 and, on the first anniversary, August 1830, but there is no intimation that Mendelssohn was yet actively working on the overture.[67]

By 12 August 1830, a few months after embarking on his grand tour, Mendelssohn had reached Vienna, and here he did renew his interest in the overture. On 16 September he could report, 'During my next leisure time I will have *The Hebrides* Overture finished, and when I think of my trip to Florence and the Tiber, the future promises to be lovely and merry.'[68] On 6 October, contemplating the overture in Graz, Mendelssohn announced his decision to change the title: 'I am working hard on my *Hebrides* Overture, which I want to name *Ouvertüre zu der einsamen Insel*. I hope it will be ready soon.'[69] Work continued on this first version of the overture (*Die einsame Insel*) in October and November in Venice and Rome; an autograph page in the Bodleian Library, which may date from October/ mid-November 1830 (no. 3), contains sketches for the recapitulation and coda,[70] and several letters from this time refer to Mendelssohn's progress on the composition.[71]

Nevertheless, the first score was not completed until early December, in Rome; on 10 December Mendelssohn wrote to his father and revealed that he would complete the overture for his father's birthday, the next day (11 December): 'For your present I will finish tomorrow my old *Ouvertüre zur einsamen Insel*; if I date it 11 December and take the bundle of pages in my hand, it will be as if I had just given it to you.'[72] Though the autograph of this first version, which may be dated 11 December 1830, has not survived, there is an undated manuscript copy in the Bodleian Library, titled *Ouvertüre zur einsamen Insel*, with some corrections possibly in Mendelssohn's hand (no. 4).[73] This source appears to transmit the earliest completed form of the overture, a version substantially longer than the printed version (323 versus 268 bars). On 16 December 1830, less than a week later, Mendelssohn completed a second version, which he entitled *Die Hebriden* (no. 5). Now preserved in The Pierpont Morgan Library, this autograph manuscript was published in facsimile in 1947.[74] Presumably this was the manuscript from which Mendelssohn played when he performed the overture in Rome early in 1831 for Hector Berlioz, who wrote in his memoirs of Mendelssohn's 'amazing capacity for rendering the most elaborate scores on the piano'.[75]

In 1948 Gerald Abraham was able to show that *Die Hebriden*, which postdates *Die einsame Insel*, is closely related to the earlier version: the two contain some parallel passages which are cancelled in *Die Hebriden*, with the result that *Die Hebriden* is 311 bars in length (versus the 323 of *Die einsame Insel*).[76] As Abraham observed, despite the cuts, *Die einsame Insel* and *Die Hebriden* are 'broadly and essentially the same'. Their differences from the final, published version lie not in the thematic contents of the overture, which by 1830 appear virtually the same as in their final state, but in the connective tissues of the work, including the bridge to the second theme, the closing of the exposition, the course of the development (considerably tightened in the final version), the retransition to the second theme in the reprise, and the coda. The alterations, summarized by Abraham and, before him, by Ernest Walker,[77] are far too numerous and complex to discuss here; however, we may consider one example, the bridge to the second theme as transmitted in nos. 4 and 5. As Ex. 8 illustrates, in the original bridge Mendelssohn introduced over a rising bass line the opening motive in two-part imitation between the lower and upper strings and then, in a thicker texture, in imitation with doublings at the sixth and third. In addition, he devised an arpeggiated crotchet figure in the winds; this, too, was presented in imitation. But in the final, printed version (bs 33–46) he pursued a more direct path to the second theme. He removed the reworking of the opening motive in favour of one rhythmically more relaxed ($\mid \, \downarrow \, \sqcap \, \downarrow \, \downarrow \mid$, taken over from b. 29). He revised the wind figure so that it descended, better to introduce the second theme in the low register of the cellos and bassoons. And above all he rejected the wealth of contrapuntal detail and removed the busy imitative writing in favour of more sparsely scored textures.

We do not know for certain when Mendelssohn began to take up these and other revisions to *Die Hebriden*, though the evidence of the primary sources indicates that he set the score aside in 1831 and returned to it early in 1832, in anticipation of a performance of the overture later that year during his second visit to England. Writing to Fanny from Paris on 21 January 1832, he affirmed his intention to recast the overture: 'But *Die Hebriden* I can't release here, because I still do not regard it as finished, as I wrote

Ex. 8 *The Hebrides* Overture (December 1830 versions), bridge to second theme

you. The middle part in D major marked *forte* is rather ridiculous, and the entire, so-called working-out tastes more of counterpoint than of train oil, gulls, and salted cod – it should be just the other way around.'[78] While in Paris, Mendelssohn showed the 'draft score' of *Die Hebriden* to Ferdinand Hiller;[79] by 23 April, Mendelssohn had arrived in London, and there on 30 April he played the work for Ignaz Moscheles. It is certain that Mendelssohn still had in his possession the 1830 score of *Die Hebriden* (no. 5), for on 1 May he presented it to Moscheles, who questioned his decision to undertake further revisions:

May 1st [*recte* 6th?] (Sunday). – Mendelssohn and Klingemann came to the children's one o'clock dinner. The former gave me the score of his overture to the 'Hebrides', which he had finished in Rome on the 16th of December 1830, but afterwards altered for publication. I often thought the first sketch of his compositions so beautiful and complete in form that I could not think any alteration advisable; during our stroll in the Park we discussed this point again to-day. Mendelssohn, however, firmly adhered to his principle of revision.[80]

By early May Mendelssohn was preoccupied with preparing a new score of the overture, as we learn from an unpublished letter of 5 May to his family in Berlin:

. . . the Hebrides beckon. I am now finishing it, that is, the fast middle section is gone, and I have to rewrite the entire score once more. That's not so easy when you think about it – a week from Monday it will be performed by the Philharmonic and a week from tomorrow is the rehearsal. Still, I'm quite happy about it. . . . My reception here has been so moving and friendly that I intend to write you all the details as soon as the copyist has the score.[81]

In all probability, the fast middle section ('eiliger Mittelsatz') is identical to the problematic 'middle part' ('Mittelsatz') about which Mendelssohn had complained in his letter of 21 January 1832 to Fanny. Comparing this passage in nos. 4 and 5 with the printed version, it is not too difficult to understand why the passage was drastically reworked. The original version (reduced in Ex. 9), which Mendelssohn described as 'noise producing' and admitted was borrowed from the *Reformation* Symphony,[82] contained a repetitive series of cadences on the mediant D major, with no fewer than three ornamented by trills. In the final version the closing passage was condensed from twenty-nine to nineteen bars, and Mendelssohn hit upon the stratagem of introducing a fresh fanfare in the winds (♩ ♫ ♩ ♩), which, concluding on the third D–F♯, enabled him to begin the development with a feigned return to the tonic B minor.

Ex. 9 *The Hebrides* Overture (December 1830 versions),
close of exposition

On 11 May Mendelssohn noted that he had 'significantly changed and improved *Die Hebriden*';[83] the work was rehearsed by the Philharmonic on 12 May and performed for the first time on 14 May with the new title *Overture to the Isles of Fingal*. Thomas Attwood, the former pupil of Mozart, conducted.[84] A second performance, led by Sir George Smart, followed at a concert of Ignaz Moscheles on 1 June 1832.[85] Of the première Mendelssohn wrote that the work was well received, though its effect was somewhat vitiated by an aria from Rossini's *Barber of Seville* that preceded it. The *Athenaeum* detected a strong resemblance to Beethoven (probably the reviewer had in mind the opening of the 'Pastoral' Symphony, whose chief motive is rhythmically similar to that of the overture) and concluded harshly that 'as descriptive music it was decidedly a failure'.[86] But the *Harmonicon* commented that 'works such as this are like "angel's visits"':

34

The idea of this work was suggested to the author while he was in the most northern part of Scotland, on a wild, desolate coast, where nothing is heard but the howling of the wind and roaring of the waves; and nothing living seen, except the sea-bird, whose reign is there undisturbed by human intruder. So far as music is capable of imitating, the composer has succeeded in his design; the images impressed on his mind he certainly excited, in a general way, in ours: we may even be said to have heard the sounds of winds and waves, for music is capable of imitating these in a direct manner; and, by means of association, we fancied solitude and an all-pervading gloom.[87]

It would stand to reason that the newly revised manuscript Mendelssohn hurriedly prepared in May 1832 was used for the first two performances of the overture. But at this point the chronology of sources again becomes skewed. On 6 June Mendelssohn wrote a letter to Sir George Smart offering the autograph of *The Isles of Fingal* to the Philharmonic Society; on 7 June, in appreciation the Society in turn resolved to offer the composer a piece of plate.[88] But this score (no. 6), if in fact it was ever presented to the Society, has evidently disappeared. Meanwhile, by 19 June Mendelssohn completed an arrangement for piano duet which has recently come to light; this autograph (no. 7), entitled *Overture to the Isles of Fingal*, was inscribed to Mary and Sophie Horsley, daughters of the glee composer William Horsley, whom Mendelssohn frequently visited in Kensington.[89] One day later, on 20 June 1832, Mendelssohn dated yet another manuscript, a full score entitled *The Hebrides* (no. 8). At some point, presumably after the overture was published in score, Mendelssohn gave this manuscript to William Sterndale Bennett, who preserved it, along with the autograph of the String Quartets, Op. 44, as a cherished memento of his friendship with the composer.[90] Though the present whereabouts of no. 8 are unknown, earlier in this century it was examined by Ernest Walker and Gerald Abraham, who confirmed that it transmitted the version of the work as we now know it, though it contained some corrections (chiefly excisions).[91]

On 10 January 1833 Mendelssohn directed the Berlin première of the overture; a review in the *Allgemeine musikalische Zeitung* referred to the work as a 'still unknown overture in B minor'.[92] A second Berlin performance in February evidently did not please; the overture, identified as 'zu den Hebriden', was described as 'too serious for the concert public'.[93] In October 1833 Mendelssohn's duet arrangement was published by Mori & Lavenu in London with the title *Overture to the Isles of Fingal*, and by Breitkopf & Härtel in Leipzig with the title *Ouverture aux Hébrides (Fingals Höhle)* and a dedication to the Bohemian baritone Franz Hauser (no. 9).[94] This publication marked the first use of *Fingals Höhle* as a title; as we shall see, the addition may have been the creation of the publisher.

On 29 November 1833 Mendelssohn sent Breitkopf & Härtel the score of his overture, presumably no. 8, in which, as he noted, 'I have still changed several things'.[95] By June 1834 the parts (no. 10) had appeared and were reviewed in the *Allgemeine musikalische Zeitung* along with the duet arrangement.[96] In the review, we find again the parenthetical reference to *Fingals Höhle*, but also this elaborate explanation for the addition to the title, linking – apparently for the first time – the overture to the cave:

Products of sound that are tied to specific subjects, and whose musical form takes shape from the contemplation and examples of these subjects, presuppose at least a general knowledge of the stimulus, so that the mood of the listener is shifted to one that to some extent comes close to the composer's during the creation of the work. . . . The splendid Fingal's Cave, pierced by the undulating sea and grandiosely adorned on both sides of its 170-foot high arch with lofty basalt columns, was believed by the Highlanders to have been built by giants for their old, legend-encrusted hero, the father of Ossian. The cave lies on the west coast of the tiny, uninhabited, treeless Isle of Staffa (that is, Island of Staves), one of many so named basaltic formations uplifted from the ocean floor. The emptiness of the celebrated island, its marvellous columns and misty beckoning from a splendid, strange, ancient time, reinforces the ghastly, sublime impression. — The title 'zu den Hebriden' is thus far too general and probably owing to the fear that only few would remember the desolate island. That can hardly be helped, and besides, every educated person knows it. Thus in listening to this music one should think of Staffa and its famous cave. All of the music bears witness to its simple greatness.[97]

By November 1834 Mendelssohn returned the corrected proofs for the score of the overture (with still final changes) to Leipzig; on 4 December, the first Leipzig performance occurred, and on this occasion, yet another title, *Ossian in Fingalshöhle (Ossian in Fingal's Cave)* was introduced.[98] But Mendelssohn, still in Düsseldorf, was not present for the performance, and the title was probably devised by Breitkopf & Härtel. From Henriette Voigt, a noted musical amateur in Leipzig, Mendelssohn received a report of the performance, which included the criticism that the orchestra concluded with a tempo faster than that established at the beginning. We have Mendelssohn's reaction in a letter of 10 January 1835:

. . . but it surprises me much to hear of my Overture in B minor being taken faster at the end than at the beginning. I suppose you mean after the *animato*? If so, I shall certainly adopt Sebastian Bach's practice, who hardly ever marked even a *piano* or *forte* on his music. I thought a *più stretto* would hardly do well, as I referred rather to an increase of spirit, which I did not know how to indicate except by *animato*.[99]

Finally, in April 1835, the score of the overture (no. 11) appeared with the title *Die Fingals-Höhle*.[100] By then, the composer's initial impressions of the Hebrides, specifically of Mull and Morven, had been supplanted by the romantic appeal of the cave and the Ossianic poems, and the labyrinthine compositional history of the work came to a close.

3

Musical influences

On 17 July 1826 the Berlin violinist Karl Möser directed a lavish benefit concert that included Beethoven's 'Pastoral' and *Wellington's Victory* Symphonies, miscellaneous part-songs for male chorus, and no fewer than three overtures, those to Spohr's *Faust* (1813), Spontini's *Olympie* (1821), and Weber's *Oberon* (1826). All three overtures were drawn from contemporary operas, a practice not at all uncommon in the Berlin concert life of the 1820s. Nevertheless, in a review of the concert an anonymous critic questioned the wisdom of transferring operatic overtures into the domain of purely absolute, instrumental music:

Like other Spontini works, the Overture to *Olympie* is often given here in concerts. But if one considers the principle that operatic overtures should be used less often for this purpose, lest their lively effect in their appropriate position – before the opera – be diminished, then we find still more reasons to argue against transplanting Spontini's overtures into the concert hall. . . . For it seems to us that Spontini has placed his overtures (especially that for *Olympie*) in such a close relationship to the operas, that we cannot possibly justify performances of them other than before the operas.[1]

'German composers', the reviewer continued, '(for example, Beethoven, Weber in his *Oberon*, Spohr in his *Faust* Overture, performed today) offer in their overtures a painting of all the essential outlines of the opera.' From the point of view of the audience, the 'work hovers before our imagination like a rhapsodic narrative; indeed, in the overture, we can already anticipate every essential element of the opera'.[2]

Among the participants in Möser's concert was the seventeen-year-old Mendelssohn, who took part as a violinist in the orchestra. Of course, just at this time the young composer was engaged with his Overture to *A Midsummer Night's Dream*, that 'boundless boldness', as he had recently described it in his letter of 7 July. But unlike the overtures performed during Möser's concert, Mendelssohn's overture from the start was conceived as an independent work – an overture, as it were, to an *unwritten* opera. Still, Mendelssohn's overture posed an aesthetic dilemma not unlike that identified

38

by the Berlin critic: to what extent could a piece of absolute, instrumental music successfully convey extra-musical ideas? Put another way, to what extent could an overture such as that to Spohr's *Faust*, conceived as part of a dramatic work and thus intended to convey a musical representation of dramatic ideas, be successfully performed and understood in a context divorced from its proper medium, the opera house?

How Mendelssohn successfully reconciled the competing demands of absolute and programmatic music in his overtures is a testament to his genius, and it underscores the significant contribution he made to the nineteenth-century German instrumental tradition. In large measure, today we view the three overtures treated in this volume as among Mendelssohn's most ambitious forays into the romantic aesthetics of instrumental music. But of course these works were not created in a stylistic vacuum; rather, they formed an extension of the nineteenth-century German concert overture, and represented an application of a new, romantic aesthetic (articulated in the Berlin of the 1820s by Mendelssohn's friend A. B. Marx) to an already established instrumental genre. Here, we shall consider the more significant of Mendelssohn's stylistic debts in the three overtures.

A Midsummer Night's Dream

We need look no further than to Carl Maria von Weber for a crucial stylistic influence on the Overture to *A Midsummer Night's Dream*. In May and June 1821 Weber had visited Berlin to conduct the highly acclaimed première of his masterpiece, the 'romantic opera' *Der Freischütz*. Not only did young Mendelssohn meet Weber at this time,[3] but he attended the performance of the opera and of another work offered by Weber, his hastily composed *Konzertstück*, Op. 79, for piano and orchestra, a seminal work that influenced the course of the romantic piano concerto and left a deep impact on Mendelssohn's own emerging pianistic style.[4] In December 1825 Weber again visited Berlin, this time to conduct the Berlin première of his 'grand, heroic-romantic opera' *Euryanthe*, and according to Julius Schubring, Mendelssohn 'frequently attended the rehearsals, and used to speak with astonishment of what the man did with a strange orchestra'.[5] By the end of 1825, Weber was already intensely at work on *Oberon*, having received earlier that year the English libretto prepared by James Robinson Planché and based on Wieland's German epic poem, *Oberon* (1780).[6] Weber survived the English première of *Oberon*, on 12 April 1826, by less than two months, and died in London on 5 June.

and___ the last faint light of the sun___ hath fled! ___

Ex. 10a Weber, *Oberon*

A striking point of resemblance between Weber's *Oberon* and *A Midsummer Night's Dream* occurs in the 'Mermaid's Song' with which the second act of the opera concludes. 'And hark! the mermaids' witching strain' (in the German, 'Zauberton', 'magic tone'), Puck says to Oberon, as the moon rises to soft horn calls and a lilting, nocturnal chorus in E major. One phrase in particular, descending scale-like from a high E (Ex. 10a), appears to have been taken over by Mendelssohn in the concluding bars of *A Midsummer Night's Dream*, where a remarkably similar figure, also in E major, descends, a *pianissimo* metamorphosis of the robust bridge theme of bars 62ff (Ex. 10b). What is more, Mendelssohn rhythmically alters the phrase by transforming the quavers into triplets, an adjustment that brings the phrase even closer to Weber's 6/8 metre. In short, one is tempted to view the resemblance as a quotation, perhaps an homage from Mendelssohn in August 1826 to the memory of the recently deceased composer.

In 1933 Georg Kinsky reconsidered this issue of a quotation from *Oberon*, but concluded that the 'borrowing' was in all probability a coincidence.[7] To support his case, Kinsky noted that the first edition of *Oberon*, a piano vocal score released by Schlesinger, did not appear in Berlin until the end of July 1826, after Mendelssohn had begun to work on the overture, and that the opera was not performed there until the winter of 1826/27, well after Mendelssohn had completed the score in August 1826. Kinsky could have reinforced his argument, perhaps, by calling on the authority of Sir George Grove, who already in 1890 had asserted, 'it is so extremely unlike Mendelssohn to adopt a theme from another composer, that we may be perfectly sure that the idea was his own.'[8]

But additional, telling evidence raises yet again the issue of Mendelssohn's debt to Weber. First, Mendelssohn's phrase is not unlike the second theme

Ex. 10b *A Midsummer Night's Dream* Overture

in the first movement of Weber's Piano Sonata No. 4, Op. 70 (1822, Ex. 10c), a work which surely Mendelssohn would have known by 1826. Weber's theme includes a deceptive turn to C♯ minor; Mendelssohn's theme wavers gently between C♯ minor and E major, a subtle reference to the ambiguous third (E-G♯) with which the overture begins.

Ex. 10c Weber, Piano Sonata No. 4, Op. 70

More striking evidence for the Weber borrowing is at hand in an unpublished Mendelssohn letter that was unavailable to Kinsky. As we know, Mendelssohn participated in the Berlin performance of the overture to *Oberon* on 17 July 1826; writing to his father and sister Fanny the next day, Mendelssohn described in considerable detail the rehearsal for the concert:

Next came the Overture to *Oberon*. With profound respect, and with some eagerness I placed my violin in its case and went out into the audience to listen for a while. It begins with a heavenly remembrance, the most beautiful opening of Weber's overtures, something like this:

etc. Soon the elves appear in the winds, the Turkish march also begins to sound, and then comes a passage in the celli and violas, as Weber often scored – but this is one of the most peaceful and noble melodies that he invented. Nothing has so enchanted me for a long time, as this melody which becomes more and more imperceptible, till it dissolves this way:

Now the Allegro streams forward; it begins with fire . . . .[9]

41

Certainly Mendelssohn's two musical quotations were notated from his recollection of the rehearsal, and so, in the second bar of the first example, after the quintessential motive of Oberon's magic horn, he inadvertently altered somewhat the voice leading of the strings. Nevertheless, the letter reveals a detailed knowledge of the opera – and not merely the overture – for Mendelssohn took the trouble to identify specific motives, first heard in the overture, that then return throughout the opera: the elves' music (Act I, no. 1), for instance, and what he labelled the Turkish march (in the final scene of the concluding Act III, heard after Oberon's farewell to Huon as the scene shifts from Tunis to the court of Charlemagne).

No great leap of faith is needed to imagine young Mendelssohn, deeply impressed by Weber's music, somehow gaining access to an advance copy of the Schlesinger piano-vocal score, noting Weber's use of a network of returning motives (a technique already familiar in *Euryanthe* and especially in *Der Freischütz*), and deciding to apply a similar procedure in his own overture to *A Midsummer Night's Dream*, for which, happily enough, a specific type of music was required to conjure up Oberon's elves, even if those of Shakespeare and not Wieland. And if Mendelssohn needed a further example of an operatic overture that exhibited recurring motives, he could have referred as well to Spohr's *Faust*, performed at Möser's concert. Not only had Spohr himself appended a note of explanation about the overture, which he described as a 'musical impression of the circumstances of Faust's life', but Carl Maria von Weber had praised Spohr's opera for its use of motives: 'A few melodies', Weber had observed, 'felicitously and aptly devised, weave like delicate threads through the whole, and hold it together artistically.'[10] The same observation could be applied to Mendelssohn's overture, and, indeed, to Mendelssohn's later incidental music to *A Midsummer Night's Dream*, Op. 61, where the proto-leitmotivic technique of the overture was more fully realized.

If Weber's *Oberon* provided an immediate source of inspiration for Mendelssohn's overture, a no less significant influence was the music of Beethoven, which more or less preoccupied Mendelssohn during the later 1820s.[11] Indeed, Mendelssohn himself appears to have cited the Overture to *Fidelio* as a kind of model for *A Midsummer Night's Dream*. During the 1840s, Johann Christian Lobe, the editor of the Leipzig *Allgemeine musikalische Zeitung*, held several conversations with Mendelssohn, which were assembled in 1855 as a sort of musical analogue to Goethe's *Conversations with Eckermann*. In Lobe's 'Gespräche mit Mendelssohn' we find this remarkable, though still little-known passage:

'Recently', I began, 'I heard your overture to *A Midsummer Night's Dream* for the first time. It seems to me to surpass all your earlier works in its originality, and I cannot compare it with any other piece; it has no sisters, no family resemblance. So one would probably be justified in saying that you have broken new ground with it?'

'Not at all', he retorted. 'You have forgotten that what I understand by "new ground" is creations that obey newly discovered and at the same time more sublime artistic laws. In my overture I have not given expression to a single new maxim. For example, you will find the very same maxims I followed in the great overture to Beethoven's *Fidelio*. My *ideas* are different, they are Mendelssohnian, not Beethovenian, but the *maxims* according to which I composed it are also Beethoven's maxims. It would be terrible indeed if, walking along the same path and creating according to the same principles, one could not come up with new ideas and images. What did Beethoven do in his overture? He painted the content of his piece in tone pictures. I tried to do the same thing. He did it in a broader overture form, and used more extended periods; so did I. But basically, the form of our periods follows the same laws under which the concept "period" generally presents itself to human intelligence. And you can examine all the musical elements; nowhere will you find in my overture anything at all that Beethoven did not have and practise, unless' – he smiled roguishly – 'you want to consider it as new ground that I used the ophicleide.'[12]

Though we must read Lobe's recollected conversations with some caution,[13] the *Fidelio* anecdote has the ring of authenticity and is consistent with what we know about Mendelssohn's profound admiration for that composer. And the anecdote invites comparisons of the two overtures, both of which are in E major. Beethoven's robust Allegro opening, interrupted twice by Adagio sections, presents an essentially circular cadential gesture: I–V–IV–I; the initial, four mysterious chords of *A Midsummer Night's Dream* (see Ex. 15a, p. 55) traverse a similar progression: I(vi?)–V–iv–I (Mendelssohn's turn to the minor subdominant may have been encouraged by Beethoven's use of iv in bs 19–20 of the *Fidelio* Overture). More telling, perhaps, Beethoven's Adagio sections, with their sustained woodwind chords, are not unlike Mendelssohn's use of sustained winds to interrupt the fairies' music. In both overtures, the juxtaposition of contrasting types of music works to establish two, separate temporal worlds. Mendelssohn knew *Fidelio* in detail already by March 1825, when, in Paris, he performed the overture at the piano for the French composer Georges Onslow, who to Mendelssohn's surprise was totally unfamiliar with the score.[14] Arguably the *Fidelio* Overture could have fired Mendelssohn's imagination in the summer of 1826, when he 'painted the content' of Shakespeare's play in 'tone pictures'.

Calm Sea and Prosperous Voyage

Undoubtedly the primary musical influence on Mendelssohn's *Calm Sea and Prosperous Voyage* was Beethoven's cantata setting of Goethe's two poems, composed in 1816, published in 1822 as Op. 112 with a dedication to the poet, and reviewed by A. B. Marx in 1824.[15] Mendelssohn may have known J. F. Reichardt's settings of the two poems for voice and piano (1809), but these modest songs offered little more than an accompaniment to the declamation of the poetry, and musically would have contained little of interest.[16] In 1828, Mendelssohn probably did not know Schubert's minimalist version of *Meeresstille* (D 216b), with a simple piano part limited to rolled semibreve chords. This setting was included in the parcel Schubert sent to Goethe in 1815, but which, on Zelter's advice, was returned unopened; it appeared in 1821 as Schubert's Op. 3 no. 2.[17]

As Marx observed in 1828,[18] Mendelssohn had dared in his overture to limit himself to the purely instrumental realm of the orchestra, in contrast to Beethoven, who had remained tethered to Goethe's texts by including a chorus. Nevertheless, the style, structure, and imagery of Mendelssohn's composition show clear enough signs of Beethoven's influence. Thus, like Beethoven, Mendelssohn set his work in D major and used the structural plan of two sections joined by a transition. Just as Beethoven had rounded out *Calm Sea* by concluding that section with a reprise of the opening bars, so near the end of *Calm Sea* Mendelssohn recalled the opening motive in the tonic (bs 25, 36ff); on the other hand, Mendelssohn expanded Beethoven's relatively compact *Prosperous Voyage* into a full-fledged movement in sonata form.

A few comparisons reveal how Mendelssohn borrowed and yet transformed certain ideas in Beethoven's cantata. First, the extraordinary openings (Ex. 11): both composers began with hushed, open-spaced sonorities sustained in the strings. Beethoven chose to emphasize the vast emptiness of the sea by omitting the fifth of the chord and superimposing two wide intervals, a tenth and an octave (perhaps an anticipation of the 'ungeheure Weite', the 'enormous breadth', in *Meeresstille*, and of the dramatic outburst in bs 27–8 of the cantata, where the entire orchestra abruptly enters to support an ungainly leap of an eleventh in the sopranos). Mendelssohn opted for a fuller chord in seven parts, yet one bounded above and below by the open interval of the fifth (the chord is actually symmetrically constructed, with 'closed' thirds in the middle, according to this pattern: 5–4–3–3–4–5). In addition, Mendelssohn indulged his painterly interests

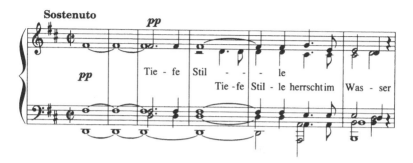

Ex. 11a Beethoven, *Meeresstille und glückliche Fahrt*, Op. 112

Ex. 11b *Calm Sea and Prosperous Voyage* Overture, Op. 27

by blending into the string sonority the dark colours of the clarinet and bassoon.

Both Beethoven and Mendelssohn extracted from these opening orchestral chords the essential thematic motives of *Calm Sea*. In the cantata, the chorus entered in b. 3 with a narrowly circumscribed figure descending from F♯; the weak third doubling in the initial string chord was reflected by the emphasis on F♯ in the chorus, where that pitch was doubled at the octave in the soprano and tenor. In the overture, the peculiar spacing of the opening chord anticipated vertically the basic melodic gesture in the contrabass, comprising a descending fourth and third (*D–A–G–F♯*), and immediately answered in symmetrical inversion by the violins (*A–B–C♯–D–E–F♯*).

From Beethoven, too, Mendelssohn probably borrowed the technique of prolonged pedal points in *Calm Sea*, and the idea of concluding the section with an unstable, open-spaced chord. Beethoven's final chord again omitted the fifth. Mendelssohn's final chord now emphasized the F♯ by placing it as the bass note of a first-inversion harmony; then, in an original stroke, Mendelssohn isolated a low A from the chord in the cellos, and set against it some figures in the winds, the first signs of the *Prosperous Voyage*. The prolonged cello pedal point effectively asserted the unstable $^6_4$ inversion of the tonic harmony; this then progressed to a dissonant, unresolved diminished-seventh chord as *Calm Sea* came to a close.

The transitional passage with which *Prosperous Voyage* begins reveals again Mendelssohn's debt to Beethoven. In the cantata Beethoven devised an instrumental transition with brisk figures in the woodwinds to suggest the gathering winds and a prolonged crescendo from *pianissimo* to *forte* to suggest the lifting of the mists and clearing of the heavens; the jubilant chorus then entered with a strong affirmation of the tonic in root position. Mendelssohn explored a similar approach, though he now took fuller advantage of the transition to convey Goethe's dynamic imagery of motion. Thus Mendelssohn dramatically expanded Beethoven's modest transition of fourteen bars to fifty bars, and prepared the inevitable assertion of the stable tonic with an emphatic (Beethovenian, one might say) pedal on the dominant. Furthermore, at the opening of *Prosperous Voyage* Mendelssohn featured exclusively the wind instruments, to which he added a serpent and contrabassoon to suggest the swelling waves; and he exploited a considerably richer harmonic palette than did Beethoven in the cantata.

In this last regard, however, Mendelssohn may have had other compositions of Beethoven in mind. For example, bars 57 and 58 contrapose a seventh chord on D in the winds against the open fifth of the subdominant harmony, G–D, in the strings (Ex. 12), a type of harmonic mixture that would have been familiar to Mendelssohn in several works of Beethoven, including the 'Waldstein' Sonata (last movement), 'Les Adieux' Sonata (first

Ex. 12 *Calm Sea and Prosperous Voyage* Overture, Op. 27

movement), the 'Eroica' Symphony (with its celebrated 'false entrance' of the horn just before the reprise in the first movement), the 'Pastoral' Symphony (opening of the finale), and, finally, the *Leonore* Overture No. 3 (near the beginning of the exposition).

The last-named work appears to have left its mark on Mendelssohn's overture in other ways as well.[19] First of all, there is the amphibrachic rhythm of Mendelssohn's bridge theme (♩ ♩ ♩ , bs 149ff), which may have been inspired by the short–long–short pattern of Beethoven's primary theme. Then there is the dramatic entrance near the conclusion of *Prosperous Voyage* of the trumpet fanfares to mark the arrival of the vessel into port and the conclusion of the voyage. A similar, and of course similarly theatrical device obtains in the development of the *Leonore* Overture, where off-stage trumpet fanfares adumbrate the arrival of Don Fernando, the rescue of Fidelio and the prisoners, and the resolution of the drama. In many ways, then, the *Calm Sea and Prosperous Voyage* Overture shows the young Mendelssohn, like Schubert during the 1820s and Robert Schumann during the 1830s, to have been a most impressionable student of Beethoven.

The Hebrides

Our third overture poses a special challenge: the search for decisive musical influences on *The Hebrides* Overture is thwarted by the unusual – and ambiguous – subject-matter of the composition (not a specific play or poem, but visual impressions of the Hebrides, and their associated folk literature) and by the extraordinary type of music Mendelssohn conceived for the score. From his letter of 21 January 1832 to Fanny, in which he decried the amount of counterpoint in the early version of the work,[20] we know that Mendelssohn's typically thorough revisions were undertaken to remove suggestions of artifice, of musical craft, in order to capture a primitive, rough-hewn quality, to grasp musically something of the desolate, uninhabited scenes he recorded in his album with Klingemann during the 1829 walking tour. In short, Mendelssohn's overture was designed from the start to be removed musically from the rich concert fare of Berlin and the established repertoire of operatic overtures then in vogue.

Nevertheless, some might find in *The Hebrides* Overture a few traces of Beethovenian influence. The defining rhythmic motive of the work which permeates parts of the overture (♪ ♫ ♩ ♩) recalls a similar figure in the first movement of the 'Pastoral' Symphony, in which Beethoven extends the figure through numerous repetitions to achieve an effect of stasis. Similarly,

Mendelssohn's broadly painted development section, with its excursions through third-related tonalities, and its static central portion (centred on the mediant D major), finds something of a precedent in Beethoven as well. Of course, the 'Pastoral' Symphony, with its vision of a utopian, unspoiled world, was the work in which Beethoven sought to achieve a special, one might say exotic, kind of music, and its culminating fifth movement, the 'Shepherd's Song' finale, undoubtedly influenced the celebratory conclusion of Mendelssohn's other major work inspired during the Scottish sojourn, the *Scottish* Symphony. In short, it is not difficult to suppose that while at work on the overture Mendelssohn had the sound of Beethoven's symphony in his ear.

But Beethovenian intimations do not account for a number of extraordinary features in *The Hebrides*: the remarkable opening, with its thinly masked sequence of parallel fifths; the decided emphasis on nuance and understatement in the overture, much of which is performed at a *piano* level; and, finally, the special type of thematicism, which occasionally brings the overture (and, again, the *Scottish* Symphony) close to the realm of Scottish folksong.

Well before he set foot in Scotland in 1829 Mendelssohn would have formed some impression of Scottish music, which, during the eighteenth and nineteenth centuries, had come to represent a musical *topos* for European composers.[21] Ignaz Moscheles concocted a medley of Scottish folk tunes in his *Anklänge von Schottland*, Op. 75, which he performed in Edinburgh in 1828. The same year Moscheles produced his *Fantaisie sur des airs des bardes écossais*, Op. 80, dedicated to Sir Walter Scott (when this work was published in London it bore the title *Sir Walter Scott's Favourite Strains of the Scottish Bards*). Like the *Anklänge*, the *Fantaisie* was written for piano and orchestra; and, as we know, one of Mendelssohn's first tasks upon arriving in London in April 1829 was to help Moscheles copy out parts for a performance in May.[22]

Mendelssohn's own first attempt to compose in a Scottish manner was the *Sonate écossaise* for piano, which appears to have been drafted for Fanny as early as 1828, thus a year before her brother's visit to the Highlands.[23] Though Mendelssohn suppressed the reference to Scotland when he revised the work in 1833 and published it in 1834 as his Fantasia, Op. 28, there can be little doubt that he originally had some programmatic purpose in mind, though exactly what that was remains unclear.

Of the three movements of the fantasy, a Scottish flavour is most detectable in the first. 'It begins', as Roger Fiske has observed, 'with some

Ex. 13 *Sonate écossaise* (Fantasia), Op. 28

preluding meant to sound like a harp, presumably the Celtic sort, and this leads into a slow movement which might well have suggested an Ossianic melancholy in Berlin.'[24] The blurred open-pedal passages, subdued, dark sonorities, open-spaced chords, and use of drone fifths are all features that could be associated with a Scottish style, and indeed that presage the style and tone of *The Hebrides*. Just how closely the *Sonate écossaise* anticipates the overture is evident at the end of the first movement, where the harp-like preluding resumes. In the concluding open-pedal passage (Ex. 13), Mendelssohn extracts from a series of arpeggiations the fifth scale degree (C♯), doubled at the octave and marked *piano*. We then hear a fragment of the first theme, echolike, and three unison tonic pitches at the end. The passage could very well have inspired the final bars of *The Hebrides* Overture, where the fifth scale degree, doubled at the octave in the trumpets and marked *pianissimo*, momentarily emerges, as fragments of the first and second themes appear in the winds; the overture, too, closes with three unison statements of the tonic.

In Scotland Mendelssohn would have had ample opportunity to hear and observe traditional music making, and the question naturally arises to what extent the music of the overture could reflect these experiences. Writing from Berlin, Zelter had encouraged his pupil to collect folk melodies during his tour; though Mendelssohn appears not to have accomplished this task,[25] we do know that in Edinburgh he attended a bagpipe competition in July,[26] and something of his exposure to folk music was recorded in the third movement of the *Scottish* Symphony, with its conspicuous pentatonic melodies. Near the Hebrides, Mendelssohn would have heard Gaelic folk-songs, including Ossianic ballads and labour songs,[27] and surely this music would have made an impression on him. But Mendelssohn appears to have maintained an ambivalent attitude toward folk music, and a sceptical attitude towards its direct use in art music. Writing from Wales on 25 August 1829, he exclaimed:

No national music for me! Ten thousand devils take all nationality! Now I am in Wales, and dear me! a harper sits in the hall of every reputed inn, playing incessantly so-called national melodies, that is to say, most infamous vulgar, out-of-tune trash, with a hurdy-gurdy going *at the same time*! It is distracting, and has given me a toothache already. Scotch bagpipes, Swiss cow-horns, Welsh harps all playing the Huntsmen's Chorus with hideously improvised variations – then their beautiful singing in the hall – altogether their music is beyond conception. Anyone who, like myself, cannot bear Beethoven's national songs, should come here and listen to them bellowed out by rough nasal voices, and accompanied in the most awkward style, and keep his temper. Whilst I am writing this, the fellow in the hall is playing

and then he varies it, and the hurdy-gurdy puts in a hymn in E flat. I am getting mad, and must leave off writing till by-and-by.[28]

Still, although he eschewed the direct quotation of folk tunes in *The Hebrides*, Mendelssohn did make certain concessions to the indigenous music of the Highlands. The opening motive, which generated the thematic material of the entire overture, describes a division of the octave according to this scheme: F♯–D–C♯–B–F♯. A few bars later the octave is divided into

Ex. 14 *The Hebrides* Overture

tetrachords: F#–C#–B–F# (Ex. 14). Both divisions resemble varieties of gapped scales common in Scottish folk music; in particular, the second became almost emblematic for Scottish subjects in European art music.[29] To be sure, Mendelssohn did not cite recognizable folk melodies in *The Hebrides* Overture. Nevertheless, he did endeavour to capture the flavour of the sounds he heard in Scotland, which ultimately determined the special character of the composition.

4

Formal considerations: a synoptic overview

Mendelssohn founded all three overtures upon the traditional principles of sonata form, yet in each case he modified the structural plan to fit the programmatic requirements of the specific subject-matter, as if to permit the extra-musical elements to vie with formal considerations. This is an approach he pursued in other overtures, for example to the cantata *Die erste Walpurgisnacht* (Op. 60, 1832, revised 1843), with its graphic interruption of the formal process to depict the transition from winter to spring, and *Die schöne Melusine* (Op. 32, 1833), with its alternating materials in the tonic major and minor for the water nymph and her knight-husband, so that the music tends toward a sonata-rondo design. Now Mendelssohn is usually not thought to be numbered among those 'progressive' nineteenth-century composers who advanced the cause of programme music – this was the composer, as Hector Berlioz put it, who studied the music of the dead too closely[1] – yet, in a curious way, his testing of Marx's 'characteristic music' in the concert overture during the 1820s anticipated Franz Liszt's comment to Louis Köhler in 1856: 'I only beg for permission to be allowed to decide upon the forms by the contents . . . In the end it comes principally to this – *what* the ideas are, and *how* they are carried out and worked up – and that leads us always back to the *feeling* and *invention*, if we would not scramble and struggle in the rut of a mere trade.'[2]

A second distinguishing feature of the three overtures – their use of interrelated networks of motivic complexes – also marks these works as among Mendelssohn's most progressive efforts. At issue here is not merely the search for proto-leitmotivic techniques, such as he would have known in Weber's *Der Freischütz* and *Oberon*. To be sure, such techniques inform *A Midsummer Night's Dream*, and allow us to assign programmatic tags to individual motives, a pastime that became all too familiar later during the nineteenth century. Rather, what sets these overtures of the 1820s apart is their systematic use of thematic transformation; their motivic-thematic complexes, in short, undergo a subtle process of adaptation and change. The technique is perhaps most strikingly evident in the coda of *A Midsummer Night's Dream* Overture, where the robust music associated with the court of Theseus (previously heard in bs 62ff, 230ff, and 586ff) is wonderfully transformed by the fairies' blessing into the nocturne-like conclusion (bars 662ff). Similar procedures of thematic metamorphosis obtain in the *Calm Sea and Prosperous Voyage* and *The Hebrides* Overtures as well, and Mendelssohn's applications of the device precede its considerably more heralded employment in such works as Berlioz's *Symphonie fantastique* (1830), or Liszt's Piano Concerto No. 1 (1849) and *Faust* Symphony (1854).

Finally, related to this flexible treatment of thematicism is Mendelssohn's conception of form as an organic process. Each overture is allowed to emerge from an initial germ cell: the motto-like wind chords in *A Midsummer Night's Dream*; the open-spaced, symmetrical chord of *Calm Sea*; and the compact, arpeggiated motive of *The Hebrides*. We are reminded of the organic process, by which the various components of each overture are inherently related, at the conclusion of the composition. All three end with subdued references to their openings, thereby returning us to their source and reinforcing the essential circularity of their design.

A Midsummer Night's Dream

In the Overture to *A Midsummer Night's Dream* a sonata form unfolds across a span of nearly 700 bars. The division of the score into a traditional ternary structure with added coda is clear enough (see Table 2), but strikingly unusual are: 1) the use of the motto (*a*), strategically placed at the beginnings of the exposition and reprise, and at the end of the coda; 2) the especially rich thematic content of the exposition, animated by no fewer than six sharply delineated figures (*a* to *f*, Ex. 15); and 3) the ever original transformations and combinations of the motives and rearrangements of their order throughout the course of the overture.

The four wind chords (*a*) are the impetus for Mendelssohn's dream-like fantasy. Embedded in the inner voices of this motto is a descending chromatic tetrachord (E–D♯–C♮– B) out of which he generates, through an ingenious series of transformations, the principal thematic ideas of the work. Thus the fairies' music (*b*, bs 8ff) alters the figure to its diatonic descending minor form (E–D–C–B); in *c*, the motive for Theseus' court, the tetrachord appears in its diatonic descending major form (E–D♯–C♯–B). Then, in the music for the lovers (*d*, bs 138ff, which A. B. Marx labelled 'das Wandeln der zärtlichen Paare'), the tetrachord is compressed to a chromatic

Table 2 *A Midsummer Night's Dream* Overture

Exposition   **Development**

First group	Bridge	Second Group	Closing					Development					
$\widehat{\overset{\frown}{a}}$	b (a')	c (f) (c') (b')	d	e		$f(c)$ f		b (a'') b horn calls	b' (a'') (c'') (d')				
I	i	I $\sim\!\sim\!\sim$	V	V		V	V	v ii $\sim\!\sim\!\sim$ ♮VII $\sim\!\sim\!\sim$ vi					
1	8	62	130	194		222		250 270 316 376					

Reprise   **Coda**

	Reprise							Coda			
$\widehat{\overset{\frown}{a}}$	b	d	e	(c')	c	f		b	$(a''')(d')$	c''	$\widehat{\overset{\frown}{a}}$
I	i♮VI	V	I	I		I	I	i		I	I
394	434	450	517	542	586	594		620	643	663	682

54

Ex. 15 *A Midsummer Night's Dream* Overture

descending third (B–A♯–A♮–G♯). Only motives *e* (for Bottom and the trades-men, bs 194ff) and *f* (Theseus' hunting horns, bs 238ff) appear at first glance to be free from the influence of the tetrachord, yet they nevertheless continue the process of compression begun in *d*. Thus *e*, for all its braying across the disjunct interval of a ninth (D♯–C♯), essentially fills a diatonic ascending third (B–C♯–D♯), and so is related to *d*; and *f* is compressed further, to an ascending second (F♯–G♯). Sharply drawn as all these

55

motives are, each enjoying its own special character, they are the product of a series of metamorphoses that traces its development from the original motto.

All six motives appear during the course of the exposition, the 'argument' of Mendelssohn's overture, with two for the first thematic group (*a* and *b*, tonic major and minor), one for the bridge (*c*, tonic major, then modulating), two for the second thematic group (*d* and *e*, dominant major), and one for the closing passage (*f*, dominant major). In drawing on this opulent, six-toned, thematic palette, Mendelssohn avoided a routine, sequential ordering in favour of an arrangement far more subtle, unpredictable, and seemingly spontaneous.

Thus *b*, which offers the first transformation of the tetrachord and projects us into the minor-keyed realm of the fairies, is penetrated by a variant of *a* (indicated in Table 2 as *a'*): twice the scurrying, staccato music of *b* is interrupted by sustained, *pianissimo* diminished-seventh chords in the winds (bs 39–40 and 56–7) that clearly borrow their sonority and register from *a*. Then, in the bridge, with the appearance of *c*, we also hear as part of the full orchestral *tutti* an anticipation of *f* (bs 70–7) that is to emerge more clearly at the end of the exposition as Theseus' horn calls. In bs 78ff motive *c* is reworked into a series of descending minim scales presented in imitation by the winds and brass (*c'*); they then yield to *b* returning in the dominant major (*b'*, 98ff). Finally, in the closing group, the hunting calls (*f*) are interrupted by a reemergence of *c* on the dominant (230ff). This continual recycling and restatement of motives in ever new contexts and combinations generates yet another level of metamorphosis in the overture, one that converts the sonata form into an ever flexible, dynamic process.

The development section is notable for its severe economy of means: here Mendelssohn seems to derive most of his material from the fairies' motive, which is employed as a backdrop to support a shifting cycle of orchestral hues. But appearances are again deceptive. Scarcely has the initial statement of *b* begun in the dominant minor (250ff) than we hear a sustained *pianissimo* wind chord, hollow and open-spaced, and thus suggesting another variant of *a* (*a''*). Unlike the exposition, where *a'* interrupts *b*, in the development *a''* is heard against *b*. More precisely, *b* is allowed to descend into the bass register, where it expends its energy as *a''* is overlaid above it. In b. 270 *b* is renewed by a fresh start in F♯ minor (ii); this time, a sustained chord appears in the low strings (bs 284–6), a delightful change in scoring that nevertheless alludes to the continuing presence of *a*. Sustained chords are now replaced by (or rather transformed into) drawn-out hunting calls echoing in the horns and by elongated pitches in the bass line, as the music reaches its point of greatest tonal instability. In b. 316, *b'* reasserts itself, now in the unexpected (though, as we shall see, carefully planned) key of D major. This modal metamorphosis precedes yet another variant of *a* in bs 322ff, and another series of transformations that ensue in bs 334–58. Here Mendelssohn compresses the fairies' music to a single tremolo in the violins on C♯. This proceeds to D in 342, and then to E and F♯ in 349 and 350; considered as a whole, the passage thus describes a considerably drawn out, ascending form of the tetrachord (C♯–D–E–F♯). The extended version of the tetrachord, of course, prepares us for the ritard with which the development concludes (bs 384ff). Nor is this the end of the magic. Against the tremolo violin figures Mendelssohn sets a descending pizzicato scale, which we may label *c″* (335ff). This scale impresses as a distant variant of the descending *fortissimo* minim scales in the bridge (*c′*), ultimately derived from *c*. With the arrival of C♯ minor, Mendelssohn brings back a motive drawn from the lovers' music (*d*, bs 168ff), now expanded to the interval of a fourth (G♯–F♯–E–D♯), transformed into the minor mode, and reharmonized (*d′*). The submediant C♯ minor harmony provides the tonal link to *a*, which now reappears in the winds to mark the reprise, and to remind us that all the marvellous transformations have sprung from those four, circular chords. But the submediant also joins the altered D major (♮VII) as a second goal in the development. In short, the principal key areas of the exposition – tonic E (major and minor), dominant B (major) – and of the development – dominant (minor), altered leading tone D, and submediant minor C♯ – derive from the tetrachord itself, yet another sign of its remarkable tonal and thematic properties.

In the reprise Mendelssohn takes special care to avoid merely retracing the thematic course of the exposition. First of all, the fairies' music is accompanied by protracted notes in the low winds, including a statement in the ophicleide of the all-important fourth E–B. What is more, the music is allowed a brief excursion to C major (bs 434ff), the altered submediant, which alludes, through another dream-like transformation, to the C♯ minor recently heard at the close of the development. Second, the music bypasses *c* and proceeds directly to *d* (bs 450ff, temporarily accompanied by *b*), and then to *e* (bs 517ff), followed by *c′* (542ff), *c* (bs. 586ff), and *f* (bs 594ff). This reordering of motives effectively delays the return to the court of Theseus, and the 'official' conclusion of the play, and continues for a while longer the interaction between the fairies and the lovers.

The epilogue-like coda draws once more on *b* (bs 620ff), but its course is interrupted by yet another transformation of *a* (*a‴*, bs 643ff). This time, however, the drawn-out wind chords chart a descending scale pregnant with motives: the scale contains two statements of the archetypal tetrachord (B–A♯–G♮–F♯ and E–D♯–C♮–B); the descending scale itself is related to *c*; and its conclusion, B–A♯–A♮–G♯, alludes to *d*. The final, breathtaking transformation of *c* (*c″*) is prefaced by four cadential wind chords (bs 658ff) that describe the progression vi–IV–I$_4^6$–V, a stable cadential gesture that now realigns the ambiguous order of the original motto – I (vi?)–V–iv–I – and asserts the subdominant in its plagal role. A series of plagal cadences announce the final resolution of the music in the strings, and Mendelssohn concludes with those timeless chords of the motto, bringing us full circle.

Calm Sea and Prosperous Voyage

To create a purely musical parallel to the static–kinetic dichotomy in Goethe's two poems was the fundamental challenge Mendelssohn faced in designing the *Calm Sea and Prosperous Voyage* Overture. At first glance his solution, a slow passage and transition linked to a ternary sonata form with added coda, may not seem especially adventuresome, but *Calm Sea*, as his sister Fanny explained to Klingemann (see p. 21 above), does not function as a slow introduction, and in *Prosperous Voyage* Mendelssohn made several adjustments to the conventional sonata-form design. The result was again an original solution that addressed the conflicting demands of musical form and programmatic content.

Calm Sea offers 'static' music on several levels. First of all, it is tonally static: the music is centred on the tonic D major; apart from a brief appearance of the dominant (b. 20) there is no prolonged departure from the tonic. Of course, stasis does not mean stability. D major appears here not as a secure tonic anchored by strong cadences, but as D major subtly destabilized by the use of first- and second-inversion harmonies, sonorities that are intrinsically related to the two configurations of the principal melodic motive, *D–A–G–F♯* (contrabass, bs 1–2) and *A–B–C♯–D–E–F♯* (violins, bs 1–5; see Ex. 11b on p. 45). What is more, at the end of *Calm Sea* there is no clear turn to the dominant, as one might expect in a conventional slow introduction. Instead we are left with the tonic harmony in first and then second inversions, perhaps an indication of the deathly calm, the *Todesstille*, that fills the becalmed sailor with fear.

Second, *Calm Sea* contains a series of four pedal points that further heighten the sense of utter motionlessness. Three are placed in the cello (bs 1–8 on D, 20–4 on A, and 41–7 on A), where their ostensible effect of placid repose is disturbed by a lower current of thematic material in the

Ex. 16 *Calm Sea and Prosperous Voyage* Overture

contrabass. The other pedal point appears in the violins doubled in octaves (bs 29–36, on D), some two octaves above a series of slight chromatic swells in the lower strings and bassoons; again, the static quality of the pedal point is destabilized by the motion of the bass line, which unfolds the dissonant interval of the tritone, B♭–E.

Finally, *Calm Sea* is thematically static: the music is filled with the contrabass motive of the first bar (*a*). As we have seen in chapter 3, the motive is derived from the opening sonority of b. 1. It is immediately mirrored by the rising line in the first violins (*a'*), and it reappears in the contrabass (b. 5), the clarinet (b. 10), and cellos (b. 12). Then, in bs 21 and 23, while its rhythmic identity is preserved, *a* is melodically reworked in the strings before its original form reappears in the violins in b. 25. After the prolonged pedal point in the violins, we hear five more statements of *a*, one after the other in successively lower registers, so that the texture is essentially suffused with the motive (Ex. 16). And, at the end of *Calm Sea*, the fluttering motive in the flute (which August Reissmann termed the 'boatswain's whistle metamorphosed'[3]) revives *a'* in its inverted arpeggiation: F♯–A–D–F♯.

Contrary to expectations, *Prosperous Voyage* begins not with the exposition proper of a sonata-form movement, but with an extended transition to suggest the gathering winds. That is to say, the onset of the exposition is delayed and thus structurally deemphasized. Without doubt Mendelssohn had before him the model of Beethoven's cantata, but he now considerably expanded Beethoven's modest transition, and, furthermore, used the section as an opportunity to draw *Calm Sea* and *Prosperous Voyage* organically together.

First Mendelssohn introduced a static *piano* harmony in the winds (bs 48ff), a clear enough allusion to the stasis of *Calm Sea*, though now the harmony is a marked dissonance,[4] and is rhythmically punctuated, first by accented minims, then crotchet triplets, and finally quavers. As the sense of motion increases, we hear a slowly descending line in the contrabass (G–F♮–E–B♭–A, bs 57–71), reinforced by the first appearance of the serpent, which also traces its ancestry to *Calm Sea* (bs 33–5 and, earlier, 16–19). An extended pedal point on A, supporting the tonic harmony in second inversion, suggests a dynamic metamorphosis of the close of *Calm Sea*. But now the unstable inversion proceeds through the dominant seventh to the tonic in root position (b. 99), and that point of arrival (an arrival denied in *Calm Sea*) finally marks the appearance of the first thematic group of the exposition.

The first theme, given to the flute (*a*", bs 99ff, Ex. 17a), is rhythmically drawn from the opening contrabass motive of *Calm Sea*; and Mendelssohn devises the theme as an antecedent-consequent group on the tonic and supertonic degrees, yet another allusion to the opening of *Calm Sea*, where the contrabass presents its motive in D major and E minor. But while the contrabass motive begins on the tonic scale degree, the flute melody of b. 99 enters on the third scale degree. This rearrangement is subsequently underscored by a *marcato* string figure stated three times (bs 107, 109, and 111, *a*''') – F♯–E–D–A – itself a permutation of the contrabass figure of bs 1–2 (with the original rhythmic configuration left intact; Ex. 17b). After another dramatic crescendo, propelled by rapidly repeated wind chords, the first theme is repeated by the full orchestra (bs 129ff) and its rhythmic figure reiterated four times in the brass (bs 141ff).

In keeping with the dynamic quality of *Prosperous Voyage*, the bridge introduces a fresh thematic transformation (149ff), but this one is now rhythmic, not melodic. Presented in the dominant A major, the bridge theme retains the melodic profile of *a*" and *a*''' by commencing on the third scale degree (C♯–B–A–E), but alters the original dotted rhythmic configuration in order to introduce the short–long–short pattern of the amphibrach (Ex. 17c). The close of the bridge, with its lightly punctuated wind tremolos and gentle *pianissimo* swells in the serpent (bs 171ff), must count as one of Mendelssohn's most imaginatively scored passages.

Ex. 17 *Calm Sea and Prosperous Voyage* Overture

The lyrical second theme (*a*"", bs 185ff, Ex. 17d), heard in the cellos and then one octave above in the clarinets, is clearly derived from the first group, and reveals again the essentially monothematic nature of the overture: the second theme reuses the dotted rhythmic pattern of *a*; furthermore, it commences on the third scale degree, suggesting *a*" and *a*"", and then rises to the fifth and tonic degrees (C♯–B–A, E–D–C♯, A–G♯–F♯), thus outlining melodically the original contrabass motive, albeit in a retrograde, *ascending* form. Much of the closing section, which describes yet another of those powerful orchestral crescendos (bs 223ff; Ex. 17e), is driven by the dotted rhythm of *a*; indeed, at the end of the exposition, we hear no fewer than eleven statements of the dotted pattern in a series of *marcato* brass fanfares (bs 243ff), a forceful intrusion that anticipates the coda of the overture.

For all its brilliance, this passage is calculated not to mark the end of the exposition but to elide with the development. There is no formal break here, no definitive cadence, but an extended diminuendo; the dominant A major is not definitively secured by its dominant, but rather approached via its subdominant, and this return of D major, and its appearance in a plagal context (D–A, or IV/V–V) reminds us of the initial plagal progression in *Calm Sea* (D–G–D, or I–IV–I); indeed, the reiterated melodic fourth, D–A, is yet another transformation, through compression, of the original contrabass motive. By thus linking the development to the exposition, Mendelssohn has once again interpreted sonata form as a flexible, organic process by which one section appears to evolve from what has preceded.

In a similar way the development begins by emphasizing its ties to the exposition; that is to say, it begins by appearing to deemphasize its developmental role. First we hear the bridge theme in the dominant (bs 271ff), and then three trumpet fanfares in D major (bs 283ff), recalling the close of the exposition. Only in bs 286ff, with the first entrance of the shrill piccolo, does the music begin to modulate and, indeed, to suggest a developmental process. The reappearance of the second theme in C major (bs 335ff) appears as a new point of departure for the development, but its true purpose is subsequently clarified by Mendelssohn's turn to G major (and minor, bs 367–78) and then, at the reprise, to D major (b. 379). These three tonalities – C, G, and D – revive the plagal relationships we have traced elsewhere in the overture and, furthermore, serve to obscure the conclusion of the development.

The recapitulation begins with yet another formal adjustment: Mendelssohn employs an inverted recapitulation, in which the second theme (bs 379ff) is recalled before the first (bs 401ff). By this stratagem, he again masks the formal articulation: the return of the second theme seems to grow naturally enough from its earlier appearance in the development in C major (bs 335ff), thereby strengthening the elision between the development and reprise.

The extraordinary coda achieves the final destination of this musical journey. It, too, is elided with what has preceded. Mendelssohn prepares the coda with trumpet fanfares articulating the all-important fourth, D–A (bs 470ff), soon taken over by the timpani and reduced to resounding strokes on the tonic D. The timpani are the agent that effects the metrical transformation from ¢ to ℃ (the metre of *Calm Sea*); the timpani also set in motion, with the ensuing Allegro maestoso, a broadly ascending scale that spans nearly three octaves and reaches its climax in b. 487, conspicuously enough, on a first-inversion tonic harmony, before cascading, descending scales bring us to a dramatic pause in b. 495. The first-inversion harmony, of course, recalls the use of that sonority in *Calm Sea*, and the energetic descending tritone of bs. 493–5 (D–C♮–B♭–A–G♯) revives a similar figure from that section (bs 32–5).

According to W. A. Lampadius, who attended Mendelssohn's performance of the overture during his début concert at the Gewandhaus on 4 October 1835, the passage in the coda represents the triumphant entrance of the ship into the harbour and the casting of the anchor; the following trumpet fanfares (bs 496ff) are shouts of jubilation (Ex. 17f).[5] But the fanfares also provide a summary of the essential elements of the work. First of all, by now adding a third trumpet, Mendelssohn is able to write full triadic fanfares in second and first inversions that underscore the role those inversions have played and that restore once again the melodic contours of *a* and *a'*. Further, the melodic contour of the fanfare, F♯–E–D, alludes to the second theme, and its dotted rhythms to the first theme.

This entire dynamic process of thematic, rhythmic, and harmonic transformations, explored so thoroughly by Mendelssohn in the overture, finds its source in the static qualities of *Calm Sea*. The three hushed chords of the concluding bars remind us of this process. These softly sustained sonorities, which describe a calming plagal progression, return us to *Calm Sea*; indeed, suspended in this comforting wash of sound in the viola part is the rising fourth, A–B–C♯–D, a subtle reference to the first violin part of bs 1–4 (Ex. 17g). Mendelssohn here seems to suggest that, as in the mysterious four chords of *A Midsummer Night's Dream*, a tetrachord – in this case, an ascending, diatonic one – offers the key to the structural plan of the work.

The Hebrides

Of our three overtures, *The Hebrides* is ostensibly the most unassuming and straightforward in formal plan: it presents a relatively uncomplicated ternary sonata form with coda. There is no separate motto to obfuscate our sense of metre and tonality, as do the four wind chords in *A Midsummer Night's Dream*; there is no inverted recapitulation, as in *Calm Sea and Prosperous Voyage*. But *The Hebrides* is hardly a conventional overture in sonata form: once again, Mendelssohn has treated the formal design with freedom so that the principal structural divisions are deliberately blurred and drawn out of focus. And the thematic process that unfolds in *The Hebrides* is again one of continuing transformation and derivation from a quintessential motivic idea.

All the principal thematic components of *The Hebrides*, including the first and second thematic groups and the accompanimental figure introduced in the cellos in b. 3, are interrelated; in fact, *The Hebrides* arguably offers Mendelssohn's most monothematic conception of sonata form. Thus the descending figure of b. 1, F♯–D–C♯–B–F♯ (an arpeggiation of the tonic harmony with the passing note C♯), generates in b. 3 its own accompaniment, which appears essentially as a retrograde version of the original germ cell (A–D–E–F♯–G–A–D, Ex. 18a). This accompaniment is allied with the turn to the mediant D major, a significant association that looks ahead to the second theme, which, when it eventually enters in the mediant (bs 47ff), is clearly heard to derive from the accompaniment of b. 3 (Ex. 18b). In just this way, then, the first subject and its accompaniment and the second subject are related to one other; one might say they seem to grow from one another, a relationship reaffirmed in the closing bars of the overture, where Mendelssohn contraposes the first and second subjects in the tonic minor (bs 265–8).

The exposition of the overture is built upon two double statements of the first and second themes, scored in each case in the cellos and first violins (bs 1 and 9, and 47 and 57 respectively). As has been examined elsewhere, the first theme is built up from the opening motive to form a three-tiered sequence, with statements on the tonic minor, mediant major, and dominant minor.[6] Such a sequential procedure and its thinly concealed parallel progressions (Ex. 18c) are extraordinary for Mendelssohn, and indicative of the artless, natural quality he wished to convey in the overture: refined thematic techniques here give way to a primitive motivic construction.

The bridge (bs 33–46), which by tradition should accomplish the modulation to the second key, appears not to function like a bridge, for the

Ex. 18 *The Hebrides* Overture

anticipated modulation is much delayed and, when it finally occurs, it is given little prominence. Most of this passage in fact aims towards the dominant F♯, and only in bs 45 and 46 does Mendelssohn finally swerve towards A, or V/III. But the diminuendo in these two bars undercuts the modulation, and the 'new' cello theme in b. 47 does not mark a clear structural break as much as it reminds us of the opening of the overture from which the theme springs.

A second unusual feature of the exposition is the closing section (bs 77–95). Based upon the opening motive, this passage builds to the first *forte* and *fortissimo* in the work, and thus disperses the subdued, brooding melancholy that has so pervaded the exposition. In addition, the closing section introduces a series of assertive brass fanfares, figures that may have some programmatic significance (see p. 82 below). But, as in *Prosperous Voyage*, the exposition is not allowed to end decisively; rather, the bright fanfares are weakened by a sudden diminuendo, and we proceed without an articulated caesura directly into the development.

Mendelssohn thus pursues the strategy employed in the other two overtures, that of eliding the exposition and development. In this case, the exposition concludes with the brass alone playing a fanfare on the ambiguous third D–F♯ (bs 93–6, Ex. 18d). A few bars before, that interval had been secured as part of the mediant, but now he exploits its ambiguity so that the development actually begins by returning to the tonic. This device is not unlike the use of the ambiguous third in the motto of *A Midsummer Night's Dream*; in that work, the interval E–G♯ is used to join the development and recapitulation by playing on the common third linking the submediant C♯ minor and tonic E major. In *The Hebrides*, Mendelssohn draws together the development and exposition via a mediant relationship.

The reappearance of the tonic B minor – and with it the opening motive in the lower strings – at the beginning of the development is another unexpected event in the overture. Perhaps Mendelssohn here intended to feign a false repetition of the exposition, a device not unlike that later used by Brahms in the first movement of his Fourth Symphony (1885). But, as we shall see, the return to B minor carries a broader meaning for the structure of the development (see the reduction in Ex. 19). Mendelssohn now directs the opening motive and the fanfares from the end of the exposition (delicately scored in individual winds) through a series of shifting harmonies that feature colourful mediant relationships. By b. 123, as he approaches the midpoint of the overture, he reaches the mediant D major and, with it, recalls the second theme. In b. 130 the music more or less

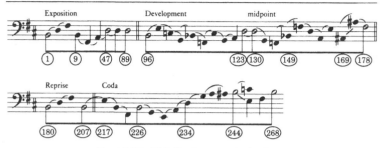

Ex. 19 *The Hebrides* Overture (reduction)

comes to a pause on the mediant and then again begins to modulate rapidly. This time B♭ minor, the lowered tonic, is briefly established. By b. 169, this B♭ is enharmonically redefined as A♯, the leading note; this directs us to the dominant F♯, in preparation for the reprise.

In effect, the principal tonal areas of the development – tonic, mediant, and dominant – recall the emphasis in the exposition on tonic and mediant, and the original sequence in the opening bars that rises by thirds from B to D to F♯. In a similar way, the dynamics of the development are coordinated to parallel the exposition: much of the section is subdued and presented in an undertone; only at the conclusion of the section does Mendelssohn build the orchestra up into a climax, the second *fortissimo* passage of the overture.

At the end of the development, this climax is erased by a rapid diminuendo (compare the end of the exposition), and the haunting first subject returns in the tonic again, as if emerging from a Hebridean mist. In bs 184–7, with the repetition of the subject in D major (parallel to bs 3–4), Mendelssohn adds brass fanfares, now a distant echo of their more resilient sound at the end of the exposition (for the possible programmatic significance of this passage, see p. 82 below). Without further ado, and without the second statement of the first theme, he proceeds to the second theme, now stated once by the clarinets in the tonic major (bs 202ff).

These thirty-seven bars (180–216) are all that Mendelssohn allots to the recapitulation, for the music now moves forward into the animated coda, the third and final *fortissimo* climax. Three sequential statements of the first theme unfold (bs 226ff), but in descending order, from tonic to submediant to subdominant (b–G–e), a counterbalance to the opening bars of the work. A brief flourish in D major restores the mediant (bs 234–7), and an abrupt turn to the Neapolitan C major (bs 249–54) postpones the final assertion of the tonic. Then, in the closing bars, a *fortissimo* conclusion is overturned by the unexpected *piano* reappearance of the first and second

67

subjects in the winds. The overture ends *pianissimo*, with plucked strings, a nuance that traces its genealogy to *A Midsummer Night's Dream* and *Calm Sea and Prosperous Voyage*, in which the unexpected quiet conclusions refer subtly to the structural circularity of the compositions.

In all three overtures Mendelssohn explored new-found freedoms in the treatment of sonata form. The adjustments to the conventional design are most readily apparent in the *Midsummer Night's Dream* and *Calm Sea* Overtures, in which details and nuances of Shakespeare's play and of Goethe's poems profoundly influenced the structural plans. In the case of *The Hebrides*, the exact subject-matter of which remains elusive and veiled, we are on a less sure footing in interpreting the formal blueprint. But the treatment of sonata form in *The Hebrides* is no more conventional than in the other members of the triptych. The deliberate elision of the structural divisions, the shifting of the structural weight by placing three *fortissimo* climaxes towards the end of the three principal sections, and the extraordinary revival in the development of the tonic and mediant tonalities (already established in the exposition) to create a certain tonal stasis – all of this is surely evidence of Mendelssohn's desire to avoid the routine and the conventional in order to suggest the exotic, the primitive, and the remote. In all three works, form is made to serve an extra-musical purpose; in all three, it is allied with the subject-matter and its various expressions, to which we now turn.

5

The overtures as programmatic music

'All pure music', Friedrich Schlegel observed in an aphorism of *Das Athenäum*, 'must be philosophical and instrumental.' Pure music engages a realm of ideas that cannot be translated into the language of mere words; indeed, 'must not purely instrumental music create its own text?'[1] In Schlegel's sketch-like comments from the turn to the nineteenth century may be found the kernel of Mendelssohn's musical aesthetic, that pure music represented a form of language superior to that of words, and that instrumental music offered the composer a powerfully expressive language to explore. At stake was the issue of what Robert Schumann in the 1830s would term the 'dependability of musical expression'.[2] Exactly what were the limits of, and how precise was musical expression? During the 1820s these issues were thoroughly pondered in the pages of the Berlin *Allgemeine musikalische Zeitung* by Adolf Bernhard Marx, the theorist who, according to Eduard Devrient, held greater sway over Mendelssohn than any of his other friends.[3]

Judith Silber Ballan and Scott Burnham have recently examined how Marx aimed at nothing less than a bold theory of 'characteristic music', by which he meant that all music expressed certain fundamental ideas, or *Grundideen*.[4] In the case of Beethoven's symphonies, music had come to express a series of powerful psychological states, which, though they could not be rendered into explicit words, could be grasped somehow at a basic level by listeners. Few who heard the 'Eroica' Symphony without knowledge of the title, for example, could fail to comprehend that the symphony expressed the heroic. Sometimes, Marx averred, an instrumental composition could successfully convey a type of musical narrative without the use of a text. One such example was Beethoven's *Wellington's Victory*, with its opposition of English and French melodies. By 1828, when Marx released a spirited defence of programmatic music (*Über Malerei in der Tonkunst*), he was able to claim that Schiller's 'Ode to Joy' could be expressed in a purely instrumental composition, without recourse to the text (Beethoven's Ninth

Symphony, which for Marx had brought the symphony into the realm of song, had received its Berlin première only two years before, in 1826).

Clearly, the young Mendelssohn was deeply influenced by Marx's ideas: our three overtures date from the period when the two friends were in closest association, and as we have seen, Marx's criticism directly influenced the course of the *Midsummer Night's Dream* and *Calm Sea and Prosperous Voyage* Overtures (Devrient even suggested that by encouraging the 'characteristic treatment' of Bottom and the tradesmen in *A Midsummer Night's Dream*, Marx was 'propagandizing for his system'). And Mendelssohn's *Reformation* Symphony (1830), with its opposition of Catholic and Protestant types of music (the Palestrinian imitative polyphony of the beginning and the incorporation of the homophonic Lutheran chorale, 'Ein feste Burg,' into the finale) seemed to invite a narratological approach similar to that Marx had applied to Beethoven's *Wellington's Victory*.[5] Finally, Mendelssohn's seven piano *Charakterstücke*, Op. 7 (1827), all of which are fitted with a particular mood for a title, could be viewed as yet another response to Marx's aesthetics of characteristic music.

Mendelssohn's own views about programmatic music were tempered by a basic belief that pure music offered an expressive language far more precise than the ambiguous language of words. Thus he steadfastly advised caution in using words to identify the programmatic content of his compositions. As we have seen, in 1833 he was reluctant to provide a detailed programmatic sketch for *A Midsummer Night's Dream*, preferring to allow the music to stand by itself. The *locus classicus* of his approach to programmatic music is found in the often cited letter he wrote to Marc André Souchay on 15 October 1842.[6] Souchay had enquired about the meaning of Mendelssohn's textless piano songs, the *Lieder ohne Worte*, and had been emboldened to suggest specific titles for individual pieces of the first three sets, Opp. 19, 30, and 38.[7] (Thus, Souchay's muse suggested 'Resignation' for Op. 19 no. 1, 'Melancholy' for Op. 19 no. 2, and, for Op. 38 no. 1, nothing less than the improbable 'Boundless but unrequited love which often turns into longing, pain, sadness, and despair, but still finds peace once again'.) Replying to this flight of fancy, Mendelssohn explained that in composing a *Lied ohne Worte* he intended no more than the piano song exactly as it stood ('gerade das Lied wie es dasteht'): what one listener might interpret as a hunting song another might hear as a devotional hymn, and so he preferred to leave the issue of interpretation, of musical meaning, to the listener.

A similar issue had arisen in 1833, when Mendelssohn was asked by an admirer in Munich, Josephine von Miller, to supply words to a *Lied ohne Worte*, probably that in A major, Op. 19 no. 4. In Mendelssohn's answer of 31 January, still unpublished, we find again a reserved tone:

You wish to have from me words for the little Lied in A major that I left for you, but how should I begin to find them? For that is the rub in such a *Lied ohne Worte*, that each one conceives its own words and sense, and allows its own interpretation. To be sure, I have done that, but only in a very rambling sort of way, here and there a word for a note, then again several notes without any words, then again words without sense; and all of this I shouldn't write to you, especially since it depends on one's own perception. Therefore, discover for yourself the verses, so that you will understand the meaning. . . .[8]

Mendelssohn's letter again reads as a vindication of music as an ultimately absolute, independent art. Yet we know that the composer allowed some *Lieder ohne Worte* to appear with titles, that he suppressed other titles, that he and members of his circle considered adding texts to the *Lieder*,[9] and, above all, that he deliberately explored the limits of programmatic music in his concert overtures. It was perhaps the overtures that Friedrich Niecks had in mind when he wrote early in the twentieth century that 'like Beethoven, Mendelssohn cannot but be regarded by the opponents of programme music as an extremely inconvenient fact. Both are classicists and producers of unexceptionable absolute music (or what is supposed to be such), and yet have not recoiled from touching the unclean thing.'[10] We shall now consider the evidence for Niecks' 'inconvenience'.

A Midsummer Night's Dream

A Midsummer Night's Dream is undoubtedly the most explicitly programmatic of the three overtures. Contemporary accounts by A. B. Marx (see pp. 12–13 above) and Mendelssohn himself identify the principal musical-dramatic elements of the composition; if that were not enough, we have confirming evidence of another kind: the incidental music Mendelssohn composed for Ludwig Tieck's production of the play in Berlin in 1843 (Op. 61). In the miscellaneous pieces that constituted the entr'acte and incidental music for this production Mendelssohn revived elements of his youthful overture, revealing *a posteriori* the dramatic source of their inspiration. *A Midsummer Night's Dream* thus permits us to scrutinize in considerable detail Mendelssohn's programmatic intentions, a luxury not provided by his other programmatic music, about which the composer usually remained vexingly silent.

In the brief account of the overture published in his memoirs (1865), A. B. Marx stressed Mendelssohn's use of characteristic music, that is, of specific motives and musical ideas meant to depict the fairies, the pairs of lovers, and the tradesmen. Mendelssohn's own account from February 1833 – begrudgingly written in response to a request from Breitkopf & Härtel – essentially confirms Marx's account, but provides additional details:

> To set forth the ideas for the composition in the programme is not possible for me, for this succession of ideas *is* my overture. But the piece is closely tied to the play, and so perhaps it might be rather appropriate to indicate the principal events of the drama for the public, so that the Shakespeare can be recalled, and some idea of the play received. I believe it will suffice to remember how the rulers of the elves, Oberon and Titania, constantly appear with all their train in the piece, now here, now there; then comes Prince Theseus of Athens and joins a hunting party in the forest with his wife; then the two pairs of tender lovers, who lose and find themselves; finally the troop of clumsy, coarse tradesmen, who ply their ponderous amusements; then again the elves, who entice all – and on this is constructed the piece. When, at the end, all is well resolved, and the protagonists leave fortuitously and happily, then the elves return, and bless the house, and disappear as the morning appears. So ends the play, and my overture too.[11]

Taking the two accounts together, we may readily identify five motives, to which we shall add a sixth, the four chords that introduce the overture (see ex. 15, p. 55). The fairies' music (*b*), of course, is the scurrying staccato figure in E minor scored for high, divided strings; Mendelssohn reused this music, more or less intact, for the concluding number of the incidental music, the 'fairy time' that marks the reappearance of the fairies after Theseus and his court have retired (the figure also appears briefly in Op. 61 no. 8). The robust music for Theseus and the court of Athens (*c*), on the other hand, is scored for full orchestra. The lyrical theme in the dominant (*d*) is designed for the 'tender lovers'; if we believe Marx, the chromatic descent suggests their wanderings into the forest. The rustic music for the tradesmen (*e*), with its ribald drones and braying figure for Bottom, was revived in the incidental music as the *Rüpeltanz* (No. 11). And the horn fanfares (*f*), for Theseus' and Hippolyta's hunting party, were also reused by Mendelssohn in the incidental music (no. 8), where they denote the pair's entrance into the forest to 'mark the musical confusion/ Of hounds and echo in conjunction' (Act IV, Scene 1).

Neither Marx nor Mendelssohn offered an explanation of the mysterious four wind chords that frame the overture and signal its recapitulation (*a*). Their threefold appearance in the overture is paralleled by three statements in the incidental music, where the chords are associated with the transformations wrought by the fairies. In the midpoint of Op. 61 (no. 6) Mendelssohn humorously reharmonizes the second and fourth chords with diminished-seventh sonorities to underscore Bottom's transformation; and the finale of no. 12, in which the fairies bless the house of Theseus (and thereby offer the final resolution of the play), begins and ends with the chords, establishing a clear parallel to the overture.

For Niecks the four chords represented the 'magic formula that opens to us the realm of fairyland'.[12] They are the agent of metamorphosis that transports us from the realm of reality to the unencumbered realm of the imagination. 'No more yielding than a dream', they are the love-in-idleness through which Oberon and Puck interact with the mortals. The chords themselves contain the seeds of change. First of all, they appear with fermatas, and are held beyond the strict time of the overture, thus negating the sense of a regular metre. The first chord is tonally ambiguous, suggesting either the tonic E major or submediant C♯ minor (a similar ambiguity, incidentally, is evident in no. 2 of Op. 61, where the opposing trains of Oberon and Titania enter in E minor and C major, or i and VI, respectively). The second and third chords progress from the dominant to subdominant, a reversal of their traditional cadential roles. And, more telling, the third chord involves a change of modality to the minor. The play on major versus minor is, of course, one fundamental type of metamorphosis that obtains throughout the overture and incidental music.

On a more subtle level, the four chords contain the basic motive – a descending, chromatic tetrachord (E–D♯–C♮–B) – out of which, as we have seen in chapter 4, much of the thematic contents of the overture is derived through a continuing process of metamorphosis.[13] Numerous examples of the tetrachord could be culled, too, from the incidental music, including, above all, its mirror inverted transformation in no. 4, to accompany the administration of the magic juice to Titania and the lovers (A–B♭–C♯–D, B–C♮–D♯–E), and in 'prime' form in no. 8, to accompany their release from its effects (the symmetrical counterpart of no. 4 – F♯–E♯–D–C♯, E–D♯–C♮–B).

A few other programmatic details of the overture may be summarized. The development, with its superbly crafted tonal, motivic, and orchestral confusion, no doubt was meant to convey the wanderings of the various parties in the forest. (At least one passage, however, was inspired not by the revelries of Shakespeare's fairies but by a fly Mendelssohn observed during the summer of 1826; he captured the buzzing insect in the descending tremolo scale for the cellos of bs 266ff[14]). The conclusion of the development, with its drawn-out ritard and otiose chords in C♯ minor, suggests the exhaustion of the four lovers, who fall asleep at the conclusion of Act III. And the remarkable coda, with its unexpected turn to E minor after the bright, 'false' ending in E major, denotes the return of the fairies at the conclusion of the play. The transformation of motive *c*, followed by soothing plagal cadences, represents the blessing of the house of Theseus: the passage reappears at the conclusion of Op. 61 to Oberon's words, 'With this field-dew consecrate,/ Every fairy take his gait,/ And each several chamber bless,/ Through this palace, with sweet peace,/ And the owner of it blest,/ Ever shall in safety rest.'

Calm Sea and Prosperous Voyage

'Perhaps in twenty years an instrumental composition will no longer be accepted unless it is legitimized through a programme.'[15] So concluded an anonymous critic of the Leipzig *Allgemeine musikalische Zeitung*, in response to a performance at the Gewandhaus by Mendelssohn of the *Calm Sea and Prosperous Voyage* Overture on 14 January 1847. A continuing – and increasingly bolder – goal of modern music, the reviewer reflected, was the use of programmatic music to introduce definite objects to the imagination of the listener, and to elicit through music the emotions that they aroused. In this type of musical description (*Schilderungsweise*) Mendelssohn was acknowledged as a master.

The division of the overture into two *tableaux* had been determined, naturally enough, by Goethe's pairing of two poems, each with its own metrical and rhyme schemes. *Meeresstille* comprises a static series of four paired couplets, regularly alternating between eight and seven feet, and regularly unfolding in a series of trochees. In *Glückliche Fahrt*, on the other hand, Goethe introduced an unpredictable rhyme scheme, and divided the ten lines asymmetrically into groups of four and six; what is more, he contracted the length of lines to six and five feet, and introduced a series of nimble dactyls to convey the new sense of motion. Dynamism thus replaced stasis, achieving an overall effect of *Steigerung*, of increasing energy:[16]

	Meeresstille	*Calm Sea*
8	Tiéfĕ Stíllĕ hérrscht im̆ Wássĕr,	Deep silence rules the water,
7	Óhnĕ Régŭng rúht dăs Méer,	Without motion rests the sea,
8	Únd bĕkümmĕrt síeht dĕr Schiffĕr	And troubled the sailor views
7	Gláttĕ Fláchĕ ríngs ŭmhér.	A smooth surface all around.
8	Keínĕ Lúft vŏn keínĕr Seítĕ!	Not a breeze from any side!
7	Tódĕsstíllĕ fúrchtĕrlích!	A dreadful, deathly stillness!
8	Ín dĕr ŭngĕheúrĕn Weítĕ	In the enormous breadth of ocean
7	Régĕt keínĕ Wéllĕ sĭch.	Not a wave bestirs itself.

	Glückliche Fahrt	*Prosperous Voyage*
6	Diĕ Nébĕl zĕrreíssĕn,	The mists are rent,
6	Dĕr Hímmĕl ĭst héllĕ,	The heavens are clear,
6	Únd Aéŏlŭs lósĕt	And Aeolus loosens
5	Dăs ángstlĭchĕ Bánd.	The anxious bonds.
6	Ĕs säúsĕln diĕ Wíndĕ,	The winds are sighing,
6	Ĕs rúhrt sĭch dĕr Schíffĕr,	The sailor is stirring,
6	Gĕschwíndĕ! Gĕschwíndĕ!	Quickly! Quickly!
6	Ĕs teílt sĭch diĕ Wéllĕ,	The waves are dividing,
6	Ĕs náht sĭch diĕ Férnĕ,	The distance is nearing,
5	Schŏn séh' ĭch dăs Lánd!	Already I see land.

Like Beethoven, Mendelssohn filled his composition with any number of descriptive musical effects to capture the imagery of Goethe's poems. Thus in *Calm Sea*, the darkly coloured low register of the opening for 'tiefe Stille', and the pedal points for 'glatte Fläche'. And in *Prosperous Voyage*, the prominent, reinforced wind section, the seemingly incessant motion in quavers, the use of circular figures to suggest the waves, and so on. But, unlike Beethoven, Mendelssohn added a substantial coda to depict the arrival of the vessel in port, a musical extrapolation of Goethe's poem, which ends only with the sighting of land. As Lawrence Kramer has observed, 'Where Goethe's text closes with an act of individuation – the speaker first says 'I' in his last line, 'Schon seh ich das Land!' – Mendelssohn's overture closes with an act of collectivisation'.[17]

With this addition Mendelssohn perhaps again came under the sway of Marxian aesthetics. In 1824 Marx had begun his review of Beethoven's cantata by considering Goethe's use of 'poetic pauses', those critical moments in a poem whose latent meaning, Marx thought, could be revealed only by a special attempt at exegesis:

There is a point in the poetic conception, where the forming imagination of the mind presses too completely, in too united and too great a way, for individual portions, individual thoughts and images to be grasped. The speech that unconsciously pours forth from the poet's lips does not completely express what moves the spirit with all its rich fullness and inner relationships; rather, that speech momentarily reveals, like the lightning of a summer night, a trace, one part of the whole. Whoever tries to read in poems of this sort only what is literally written, is deceived in imagining to have understood the poetry. Only a tested art of exegesis supported by psychology can sometimes fill these poetic gaps; and only one's own ability to have a poetic presentiment can always accomplish this task.[18]

According to Marx, Goethe's poetry was replete with pauses containing latent meaning. In the case of *Meeresstille*, Marx believed that the deathly terror of the becalmed sailor (*Todesangst des Einsamen*) – not the descriptive imagery of the verses – represented the soul of the poem. And because poetry was an ethereal art of ideas – a kind of 'bodiless' art – the powers of the composer could be marshalled somehow to bring us closer to the realm of poetic presentiments, to fill in those poetic pauses with a new, musical substance. Thus Beethoven had surpassed the achievements of his predecessors by enabling music to penetrate the furthest boundaries of poetic intuition and silence. And so, instrumental music could illuminate additional parts of the whole, could capture compellingly in purely musical terms the essential *Grundideen* of the poetry.

Mendelssohn appears not to have revealed his programmatic intentions for the overture, but this reticence did not prevent his contemporaries from probing its meaning. Three little-known accounts provide some intriguing clues. Julius Schubring, for example, recorded this amusing anecdote about the second theme in *Prosperous Voyage*:

In the *Meeresstille und glückliche Fahrt* Overture, there is a most charming melody serving to reintroduce the first notes of the introduction; it begins on the third, then rises to the fifth, and ends upon the octave. I told Mendelssohn that it suggested to me the tones of love, which, thanks to the prosperous voyage, is entranced at approaching nearer and nearer the goal of its desires. He said that such was not his notion in composing it; he had thought of some good-natured old man sitting in the stern of the vessel and blowing vigorously in the sails, with puffed-out cheeks, so as to contribute his part to the prosperous voyage.[19]

(As we know from the memoirs of Gustav Droysen, this cello melody, which appears as the second theme of the exposition (bs. 185ff), became a form of salutation among the composer's friends in Berlin.[20]) From Ernst Pfundt, Mendelssohn's timpanist in the Gewandhaus orchestra and the author of a treatise on the instrument, we learn that the timpani strokes in the coda near the end (bs 475ff) were meant to represent volleys of cannons greeting the arrival of the vessel in port.[21]

Finally, Mendelssohn's performance of the overture at the Gewandhaus in January 1847 prompted a detailed review in the *Signale für die musikalische Welt*, and here there is an extended programmatic interpretation, which is quoted in full:

Also the still, motionless sea that quietly, like a child of the cloudless heavens, mirrors the deep blue, is unending in its beauty. One must have seen it, as it kisses the gulf of Spezzia fragrant with oranges, or as it rests on Parthenope's bosom in the moonlight, to grasp the poetry of this peace and stillness, which the composer of *Calm Sea and Prosperous Voyage* has reproduced so charmingly and pleasantly in his ethereal tones. Now for the sailor, who is held in his ship motionless on the smooth mirror, this peace is stressful and unwelcome. But, hark! from the distance the first gentle wind begins to murmur, and to fold the smooth surface, and soon there arises a fresh breeze, so that the waves begin to dance in a merry tempo and to lift up their foam-crowned heads. Already the foresail is full; already the great sail, that had just hung dangling, is inflated. The busy hands of the sailors make haste, obeying the welcome call of their captain, and set the other sails; and now the ship glides quickly and proudly through the rising motion of the swells, pitching toward the longed-for friendly coast. A threefold cry of jubilation greets the land; thundering shots of salutation answer from the shore. Now just a few strong stretches, and the ship is in port, and with a joyful, thankful glimpse to heaven those safe from danger disembark. This is Mendelssohn's *Calm Sea and Prosperous Voyage*, the most fortuitous and noble piece of tone painting created in recent times. It always summons up in us the same images and yet remains forever new to us. Through gradations of the most varied emotions it arouses our feeling of sympathy to jubilation; it leaves behind a sense of satisfaction, as we can only enjoy in a thoroughly beautiful work of art. And, through its changing phantasy that animates the subject, and through its fine, poetic fragrance poured out over the work, it appears to us to have surpassed even Beethoven's conception of the same subject, although Beethoven (admittedly observing the requirements of the cantata), remained more faithful to the character of Goethe's texts.[22]

The *Signale* account confirms and elaborates Pfundt's interpretation of the coda. The timpani cannonade, we are told, is answered by a threefold cry of jubilation from the ship; no doubt, this is the unexpected introduction of the three trumpets in bs 496ff (see Ex. 17f, p. 61). But what remains unexplained is the extraordinary conclusion of the overture, which Tovey described as a 'poetic surprise of a high order'[23] – the three sustained chords that bring us back to the opening of *Meeresstille*, suggesting that, for Mendelssohn,

Goethe's voyage is ultimately a circular, self-renewing act of discovery. In this concluding plagal cadence, which indeed leaves us with a feeling of satisfaction, we discover the final resolution of the *Todesangst* Marx had identified as the crux of *Meeresstille*. And in these concluding chords we have, perhaps, Mendelssohn's final attempt to fill Goethe's poetic gap.

The Hebrides

Unlike its siblings, *The Hebrides* Overture has more or less successfully resisted attempts at a detailed programmatic interpretation. Apart from the curious change in titles, Mendelssohn left no compelling clues about his intentions. There is, of course, no play, no poem that served as the direct inspiration for the work; rather, the overture became the musical receptacle for Mendelssohn's visual impressions of Scotland. Image became sound, and we can perhaps attribute this remarkable masterpiece to an ultimately unfathomable process of synaesthetic transformation.

The visual impetus played a crucial role in Mendelssohn's music.[24] Indeed, we should remember that the sketch pad and watercolours were Mendelssohn's constant companions, that his *Reisebriefe* are filled with detailed, quasi-photographic descriptions of the landscapes and scenes he encountered during his travels, that he was familiar and experimented with productions of *tableaux vivants* accompanied by music (indeed, Fanny referred to the *Calm Sea and Prosperous Voyage* Overture as two tableaux),[25] and that several of his compositions celebrate the painterly, the visual. Thus, for Leon Botstein, in *Calm Sea*

the visual imagery again frames the musical form. Mendelssohn was able to depict the sense of distance, color, light, and three-dimensional space through orchestration. The sections of the work follow as would a series of sequential paintings, which do more than chronicle action.[26]

In a similar way, *The Hebrides* Overture could be 'seen' as a musical rendering of the visual stimuli impressed upon Mendelssohn as he surveyed the Hebrides from Oban. Whereas the dramatic content of Shakespeare's comedy and the process of *Steigerung* in Goethe's poems (*pace* Botstein's emphasis on the visual) inspired types of musical narratives in *A Midsummer Night's Dream* and *Calm Sea and Prosperous Voyage*, *The Hebrides* stands as the overture most heavily dependent on the visual for its inspiration and meaning. Thus, Edward Lockspeiser, for whom the overture was 'one of the first examples of musical Impressionism', emphasized its painterly elements, the remarkable way, for example, in which Mendelssohn extracted from a traditional, classical orchestra delicate nuances and shades of colour.[27] Indeed, in its orchestral indistinctness (the faint *pianissimo* trumpets that briefly emerge through the *fortissimo* bars near the end are one exquisite example) Lockspeiser found a compelling parallel to the art of Turner, whose own contemporary painting of Staffa (*Staffa, Fingal's Cave*, 1831), criticized for its vagueness, elicited from the artist the worthy rejoinder, 'Indistinctness is my forte.'

Despite the attraction of interpreting *The Hebrides* as a musical master-piece of a landscape painter of the first order (Wagner's formulation to Edward Dannreuther), we should remember that Mendelssohn was not immune to other, literary stimuli that may have affected his concept of the overture. In particular, in coming to Scotland in 1829, both Mendelssohn and Klingemann would have been attracted by the poetry and novels of Sir Walter Scott, and in making the difficult journey to Staffa and Fingal's Cave, they would have been equally aware of its association with Ossian, specifically the epic poem *Fingal*, published by James Macpherson in the 1760s. Thus there remains the possibility that in *The Hebrides* Overture 'the poetic was mediated through the visual into the musical'.[28]

Of course, by the 1820s Macpherson's purported translations from the Gaelic of allegedly third-century Celtic epic poetry had been commonly debunked as a literary forgery (in the eighteenth century Samuel Johnson, for one, had already labelled Macpherson an 'imposture from the beginning'[29]). If, during the eighteenth century, the Ossianic poems had offered Johann Georg Sulzer a rich alternative to the classical epic tradition, if 'Fingal was the better Achilles',[30] by the nineteenth century many critics had recognized Macpherson's handiwork for what it actually was – a concoction freely prepared from Ossianic fragments with liberal appropriations from Homer, Virgil, and all the rest. And yet the fascination with Ossian as the noble art of a primitive people endured, especially on the Continent. In Germany the appeal of Ossian was owing in part to Herder's belief that in the poems lay the sources of German folk poetry, and in part to the translations of Ossian that Goethe incorporated into his sensational novel, *The Sorrows of Young Werther* (1774). Perhaps understandably, then, Ossian still struck a resonant chord in Mendelssohn's companion Klingemann in 1829. And so, after visiting Iona, he noted, 'there is truly a very Ossianic and sweetly sad sound about that name'.[31]

In the case of Sir Walter Scott, Mendelssohn and Klingemann were drawn to a living literary celebrity, albeit a celebrity whose full identity had only recently been appreciated. Established first as the poet of long narrative ballades, including *The Lady of the Lake* (1810, the inspiration for Rossini's opera of 1819, *La donna del lago*), Scott had begun in 1814 to release anonymously his long series of historical romances, the *Waverley* novels. But in 1826, with the failure of his publisher, the authorship of the 'Great Unknown', the 'Wizard of the North', was disclosed. At the end of July 1829 Klingemann and Mendelssohn travelled to Abbotsford, Scott's recently constructed manor (described by the American writer Washington Irving as a 'huge baronial pile'[32]), but were only able to engage the author in 'at best one half-hour of superficial conversation' (for his part, Scott left no record at all of the meeting in his journal).[33] Nevertheless, Scott's works were well known to the Mendelssohn family: both Fanny and Felix set texts from *The Lady of the Lake* (including the celebrated 'Ave Maria'); we have a report of their mother, Lea, reading *Ivanhoe* (though she appears to have preferred James Fenimore Cooper);[34] and several of Scott's works appear in a list Mendelssohn compiled of his library in 1844.[35] In Germany, where translations of the *Waverley* novels in pirated editions were eagerly awaited during the 1820s, and where hack writers produced derivative subliterary novels, Scott's international influence was at its zenith.[36] Not surprisingly, then, we find several allusions to Scott in Klingemann's letters from 1829, including this observation as the two travellers returned from the Hebrides in August 1829: '. . . we start for Loch Lomond and the rest of the scenery which ought to be published and packed up as supplements to Sir Walter Scott's complete works'.[37]

Mendelssohn himself seems not to have mentioned Scott and Ossian in the meticulous letters he sent to Berlin in 1829, yet that does not necessarily mean that he escaped their influence when he composed the overture. There is no question here of a programme as detailed as those for *A Midsummer Night's Dream* and *Calm Sea and Prosperous Voyage*. *The Hebrides* is programmatic in an implicit rather than an explicit manner, a quality that it shares with its enigmatic relative, the *Scottish* Symphony. And yet there is the intriguing evidence of Mendelssohn's titles, evidence that admittedly poses more questions than answers, but that may offer some crucial clues about the composer's purpose. Beginning with *Die Hebriden* (1829), Mendelssohn proceeded to *Ouvertüre zur einsamen Insel* (1830), *The Isles of Fingal* (1832), and *Fingalshöhle* – the last most likely at the encouragement of his publishers, Breitkopf & Härtel (see pp. 35, 36). The progression suggests a gradual narrowing of the overture's scope, from the general geographical region of the Hebrides to the cave on Staffa. In addition, *The*

Isles of Fingal and *Fingalshöhle* introduce and strengthen the association of the overture with Ossian.

But what of the *Ouvertüre zur einsamen Insel?* This could simply connote the romantic fascination with an exotic locale, or it could refer specifically to Staffa. Or it could suggest Macpherson's Ossianic poems: in Book II of *Fingal*, for example, Cuthullin describes the approaching fleet of Fingal as 'the ships of the lonely isles'. Finally, the title could allude to the second canto of Sir Walter Scott's *Lady of the Lake*, entitled 'The Island'. Though the canto describes the remote hiding place of Helen and Douglas, outcasts from the court of James V of Scotland, and thus historically distanced from Ossian, the poetry impresses upon us the image of the 'lonely isle' as a recurring refrain; what is more, the image is associated with a song performed by the harper Allan-Bane, a mysterious, bard-like figure.[38] In short, the range of titles presents a multiplicity of interpretations, and it may well be that in his overture Mendelssohn was attempting to capture musically something more than a landscape or seascape, something more than 'a reverie perfumed with rural fragrances from the Scotch mountains', as one reviewer described the work in 1847.[39]

In the early nineteenth-century European imagination, Ossian was not infrequently invoked in unusual contexts. Thus in *René* (1802) Chateaubriand contrived to have the bard appear in the wilderness of America, and Stendhal, attending the première of Rossini's *Donna del lago*, offered this confused description of the opening scene:

a wild and lonely loch in the Highlands of Scotland, upon whose waters the Lady of the Lake, faithful to her name, was seen gliding gracefully along, upright beside the helm of a small boat . . . The mind turned instantly towards Scotland, and waited expectantly for the magic of some Ossianic adventure.[40]

For Mendelssohn to have combined in the overture visual impressions with literary recollections of Scott and Ossian would not have been inconsistent with the European fascination for Scotland at that time.

Finally, there is compelling evidence that *The Hebrides* was understood by Mendelssohn's contemporaries to convey an Ossianic quality. After the first Berlin performance of the work, on 10 January 1833, a reviewer wrote:

Herr Felix Mendelssohn Bartholdy's third concert began with a still unknown overture in B minor, which the composer had sketched *in situ* during his visit to the Hebrides Islands, and whose character bears the wild romantic quality of those islands that inspired Ossian to his poems.[41]

Julius Benedict, the pupil of Weber and friend of Mendelssohn who produced one of the first biographies of Mendelssohn in 1850, went even further; the overture, he asserted, was

perfectly different from its predecessors, but replete with exquisite touches of feeling and musical expression. One might fancy that one heard, now the lament of Colma on the solitary shore, now the passionate accents of Fingal, or again, the strife and din of the distant battle.[42]

And finally, in December 1834, for the Leipzig première of the work, the overture was billed as *Ossian in Fingalshöhle*.[43] Not surprisingly, as we shall see in Chapter 7, the overture heavily influenced Niels Gade's Op. 1, the *Echoes of Ossian* Overture, a work that won acclaim at the Gewandhaus during the 1840s.

But what of Mendelssohn's music in the overture? The extraordinary style of the piece suggests that Mendelssohn was intending to capture a primitive, folk-like type of music, one, as he put it, that favoured sea gulls over counterpoint. The striking voice-leading of the opening, with its progression by direct fifths (see Ex. 18c, p. 65) – a progression that Mendelssohn ordinarily would have taken great pains to avoid – certainly evokes the primitive, the uncultured. Could this represent an attempt to suggest the Ossianic? Equally compelling for our investigation are the D-major brass fanfares with which the exposition closes, fanfares that could bring to mind the epic battles of Fingal (Ex. 18d, p. 65). Stated *fortissimo*, these fanfares are allowed to proceed directly into the development, and through a series of *diminuendos* and rescorings in the woodwinds their power is vitiated. Indeed, the effect of the first part of the development is to negate the brilliant, brassy sound of the fanfares, rendering them nothing more than a fleeting memory. In b. 186, just after the beginning of the reprise, additional fanfares are heard in the brass, but now marked *piano*. As we now know, those fanfares indeed carried a military connotation for Mendelssohn. He quoted them in a clear enough context in the song 'Wenn die Abendglocken läuten' from his charming Singspiel, *Die Heimkehr aus der Fremde*, composed in 1829 for his parents' silver wedding anniversary and published posthumously as Op. 89 (Ex. 20a–b). The song is sung by the soldier Hermann, returned (like Mendelssohn) from abroad, who recalls how he thought of his beloved Elizabeth while he was assigned sentry duty on a 'forlorn post'. Quite possibly these fanfares in *The Hebrides* suggested to Benedict the 'passionate accents of Fingal', and the 'strife and din of the distant battle'.[44]

doch der Sol - dat drauss' im weit- en___ Feld

Ex. 20a *Die Heimkehr aus der Fremde*, Op.89

We will never know for certain the full extent of Mendelssohn's programmatic intentions in *The Hebrides*. The work remains protected by its shadowy sonorities, and yet it arouses a variety of interpretations. Its hypnotic mood conjures up a musical fantasy, in which various elements, now visual, now literary, freely co-mingle. If *The Hebrides* offers the most elusive of Mendelssohn's overtures, it nevertheless reveals the fundamentally romantic nature of his aesthetic approach to the genre.

Ex. 20b *The Hebrides* Overture

6

Some thoughts on Mendelssohn's orchestration

According to conventional wisdom Mendelssohn did not achieve significant innovations in the art of orchestration. As a cursory review of his scoring practices confirms, he relied for the most part upon the classical orchestra of Beethoven, with occasional additions, usually designed to underscore a special effect or programmatic idea. In the woodwind, Mendelssohn customarily limited himself to paired instruments. Exceptions to this rule include the addition of the piccolo in *Prosperous Voyage* (to suggest the gathering force of the wind) and in *Die erste Walpurgisnacht*, where the instrument's shrill accents are associated with the pagan Druids, and the use of the contrabassoon and serpent, again in *Prosperous Voyage*, to suggest the depth and broad expanse of the sea (the serpent also appears in the oratorio *St Paul* to reinforce the bass line).

In the brass, Mendelssohn typically scored for paired horns and trumpets; an early exception includes the opera *Die Hochzeit des Camacho* (1827), in which an expanded brass section (four horns, two trumpets, and three trombones) announces the knight-errantry of Don Quixote. Four horns are also required in the *Ruy Blas* Overture, *Lobgesang* and *Scottish* Symphonies, and in *Elijah*. Trumpets appear in pairs in Mendelssohn's scores, except in the coda of *Prosperous Voyage*, in which a third trumpet is added to bolster the *Jubelruf* as the vessel approaches the safety of the harbour. As for trombones, Mendelssohn generally reserved them for ceremonial or religious contexts, as in the *Reformation* Symphony, Psalm 91 Op. 98 (1844), *Die erste Walpurgisnacht*, the *Lobgesang* (where they present in responsorial fashion the opening intonation), and *Elijah* (where their strident tritones are associated with the curse enunciated at the beginning by the prophet). Mendelssohn did not live long enough to witness the tuba established in the orchestra and did not write for that instrument; however, as we have seen, he did use the ophicleide with great effect in *A Midsummer Night's Dream* (and incidental music); the ophicleide is also used to reinforce the bass line in *Elijah*.

As for percussion, Mendelssohn rarely exceeded the use of two timpani; only rarely did he add extra percussion instruments. In *Die erste Walpurgisnacht*, the bass drum and cymbals invoke the sound of a Janissary band to support the assault of the pagan Druids on the Christians, and – extraordinary for Mendelssohn – in the second act of *Die Hochzeit des Camacho* a complement of triangle, tambourine, cymbals, and bass drum lends local colour to the Spanish bolero and fandango. The harp makes but few appearances in Mendelssohn's music; these include the music to *Athalia* (1843) and Psalm 91, where the instrument is mandated by the text 'Lobet den Herrn mit Harfen'. With respect to the string section, Mendelssohn almost always scored for five-part strings with the cellos and contrabass divided (the early string *sinfonie* of 1821–3 display primarily four-part writing). Exceptions to this rule include the unusual division of violins into four parts for the fairy music in *A Midsummer Night's Dream* and the use of divided violas and cellos in the sacred cantata *O Haupt voll Blut und Wunden* (1830) and in *Verleih uns Frieden* (1831).

Mendelssohn's modest demands for orchestral resources contrast strikingly with those of his contemporary Berlioz, whose pioneering *Grand traité d'instrumentation et d'orchestration modernes*, which began to appear during the 1840s, is fraught with suggestions for novel orchestral effects and combinations and detailed commentary devoted to 'modern' and unusual instruments. In Mendelssohn's view Berlioz's striving for novel orchestral devices represented an exercise in exaggeration. Here, for example, is Mendelssohn's reaction to the finale of Berlioz's *Symphonie fantastique*, communicated in a private letter of 15 March 1831 to his family in Berlin:

cold passion represented by all possible means: four timpani, two pianos for four hands, which are supposed to imitate bells, two harps, many large drums, violins divided into eight different parts, two different parts for the double basses which play solo passages, and all these means (which would be fine if they were properly used) express nothing but complete sterility and indifference, mere grunting, screaming, screeching here and there.[1]

For all their reactionary tone, these comments conceal the central role that orchestration *did* play in Mendelssohn's own music: though he deliberately restricted his orchestral means, preferring to work with a traditional double woodwind orchestra, Mendelssohn was able to achieve a remarkable richness of orchestral colour and, indeed, to create highly original applications of orchestral nuance. Despite the conservative appearance of his scores, orchestration was most certainly a fundamental aspect of the compositional process.

We need look no further than the August 1829 sketch for the opening of *The Hebrides*, filled with detailed orchestral cues which reveal the fundamental role of orchestal colour in the compositional process *ab initio* (see Ex. 7, pp. 28–9).

Mendelssohn's sensitivity to orchestral colour was no doubt related to his interest in painting and drawing; this is apparent most clearly, perhaps, in *The Hebrides*, where his visual impressions of Scotland had a profound impact upon the musical imagery of the overture. From A. B. Marx we have this confirming evidence that Mendelssohn approached the art of orchestration as a painter selecting mixtures of colours from a palette:

> But even verbal exchanges between the two of us, whose lives had grown together so closely, could easily take on strange forms, particularly when they turned to subjects like instrumentation that do not permit an exact designation. I can still remember the astonishment in Droysen's look, during a visit to my room, when he overheard me saying to Felix, 'Here pure purple would have to be used; the horns were dampening the splendour of the trumpets'; and Felix replied, 'No! No! That shouts too loudly; I want violet.'[2]

We can only conjecture about the identity of the orchestral passage Marx challenged, though our three overtures date from the time Mendelssohn, Marx, and Droysen spent together in Berlin and offer several possibilities: for instance, the hunting calls in bs 222ff of *A Midsummer Night's Dream*, with the trumpets doubled by horns; the *Jubelruf* in the coda of *Prosperous Voyage*, first introduced by the three trumpets but then taken over by horns and winds in bs 505ff; and the quotation from *Die Heimkehr aus der Fremde* near the start of the recapitulation in *The Hebrides* (bs 186–7), in which blended horns and trumpets perform *piano* fanfares.

Indeed, the three overtures teem with highly specialized applications of orchestral colour, extracted, for the most part, from a rather conservative double woodwind, double brass orchestra. True, Mendelssohn does indulge in some unusual devices in orchestration. These include, in *A Midsummer Night's Dream*, in addition to the division of the violins *a 4* and use of the ophicleide mentioned earlier, the pointillistic applications of a solo contrabass and solo cello in the development (bs 276–8), and, in *Calm Sea and Prosperous Voyage*, the additions of the serpent, contrabassoon, piccolo, and third trumpet. All of these examples may well reflect Mendelssohn's response to Marx's spirited arguments during the 1820s for 'characteristic' music, by which he meant programmatic music with sharply delineated motives that could carry extra-musical meaning.

For Mendelssohn, orchestration served as a primary tool that helped to draw into clear focus the various extra-musical elements of his overtures. Thus, in *A Midsummer Night's Dream*, the divided violins *a 4* (high register, *pianissimo*, and staccato) can only connote the fairies; the motto–like wind chords (expanding across several registers, *piano*, and sustained in an ametrical fashion) contain the essential element of metamorphosis through which we enter and leave the Shakespearean realm, and so on. By sharpening the distinction between orchestral colours (and, no less important, modes of articulation), Mendelssohn enables us to re-experience through his musical lens the dramatic elements of Shakespeare's play. The central role of orchestration in this process is thus manifest.

In many ways the orchestral conception was in fact crucial to Mendelssohn's creation of the three overtures. Three brief examples serve to underscore this point. In *A Midsummer Night's Dream*, the four, motto-like wind chords appear three times, each with subtle (and easily overlooked) changes in scoring. The first statement is scored for winds alone. The second, heard at the reprise (bs 394–403), is virtually the same, but with the fourth chord Mendelssohn adds divided violins, blending their E major sonority into the winds before resuming the fairy music in E minor. And finally, at the conclusion of the overture, he introduces some new inflections: the third and fourth chords are respaced (yielding in the flutes the open sixth B–G♯, instead of the original third, E–G♯), and a timpani roll on the dominant is added – 'one of the most consummate subtleties to be found in any orchestration', according to Tovey.[3] In this way the very motto itself undergoes a wonderful process of metamorphosis, and orchestration is the means used to effect the ever so subtle transformations.

In *Calm Sea and Prosperous Voyage*, Mendelssohn used a variety of open-spaced sonorities to convey the sublime expanse of the sea. This process

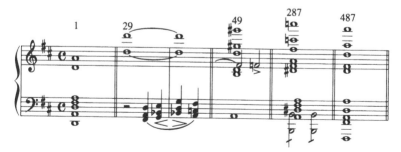

Ex. 21 *Calm Sea and Prosperous Voyage* Overture

87

begins at the opening of *Calm Sea*, with the *Urmotif* placed in the depths of the contrabass. Further on in *Calm Sea* (bs 29ff), against a sustained octave pedal point in the violins, he places a series of sixth chords two octaves below, thereby emphasizing the extremes of the orchestral compass, and leaving the middle register empty. Ex. 21 summarizes some of these open-spaced scorings, including one in the development that utilizes the piccolo.[4]

Finally, orchestral colour is an active agent in *The Hebrides*. The opening passage, rising sequentially by thirds (bs 1–8) and then repeated (bs 9–16), reappears at the beginning of the reprise (bs 180ff), and returns with modifications in the coda (bs 226ff), where Mendelssohn redirects the sequence to *descend* by thirds. Through these four statements of the sequence we 'hear' a shifting series of orchestral hues in the accompaniment: in the opening bars, sustained brushes of violins, clarinets, oboes, and flutes; in the repetition, horns and trumpets; in the reprise, shimmering trills and tremolos in the violins, clarinets, and flute; and, finally, in the coda, sustained, *fortissimo* octave doublings in the winds. Again, Mendelssohn regulates the orchestration to derive ever changing colours from the winds, brass, and strings; and it is this process, in the last analysis, that obscures the barrier between musical and visual imagery and evokes the synaesthetic, romantic qualities of the overture.

7

Influence and reception of the overtures

To a large extent the critical reception of Mendelssohn's three overtures paralleled the general reception of the composer, though ultimately the overtures survived the shifting tides of his posthumous fortune to become a cornerstone of his contribution to nineteenth-century romanticism. In Germany and England Mendelssohn's unexpected death in 1847 at age thirty-eight was viewed as an international tragedy, and he was soon memorialized by a remarkably ardent hero-worship usually only accorded dignitaries of the highest rank. The first wave of this adulation crested in 1853, when Elizabeth Sheppard published the novel *Charles Auchester*, freely based on the life of Mendelssohn, who appeared in its pages idealized as the Chevalier Seraphael.[1] In the fifth chapter of the second volume Sheppard describes an opera, suspiciously similar to the music to *A Midsummer Night's Dream*, as the very embodiment of the Chevalier's art of 'blissful modulations'. No title is given for the opera, though its libretto is freely drawn from Shakespeare's *The Tempest* and *A Midsummer Night's Dream*. As the curtain goes up – *before* the overture – Ariel ('the Ariel of our imaginations, the Ariel of that haunted music') delivers a prologue. Ariel's soul is 'native with the spheres/ Where music makes an everlasting morn'. And now he longs to 'disenchant/ My most melodious treasure breathless hid/ In bell and blade'.

At Ariel's invocation of music to 'dawn on the dreamland of these alien dells!' the overture commences, and it soon becomes clear that the Chevalier's overture is a thinly disguised reworking of the Overture to *A Midsummer Night's Dream*, as revealed to us through the roseate filter of Sheppard's highly sentimental prose:

Three long, longing sighs from the unseen wind instruments, in withering notes, prepared the brain for the rush of fairy melody that was as the subtlest essences of thought and fragrance enfranchised. The elfin progression, *prestissimo*, of the subject, was scarcely realized as the full suggestion dawned of the leafy shivering it portrayed. The violins, their splendours concentrated like the rainbows of the dewdrops, seemed but the veiling voices for that ideal strain to filter through; and yet, when the horns spoke out, a blaze of golden notes, one felt the deeper glory of the strings to be more than ever quenchless as they returned to that ever-pulsing flow.

After the overture, we hear a duet for Titania and Oberon, and then a 'fairy march *pianissimo* – a rustling, gathering accompaniment that muffled a measure delicate as precise' – an unambiguous reference to the fairies' march in Mendelssohn's incidental music for *A Midsummer Night's Dream*, Op. 61 no. 2. The opera concludes with a 'final chorus in praise of wedded love' that rises 'chime upon chime from the fairy voices and the rapt Elysian orchestra', again, not far removed from the finale of Mendelssohn's incidental music. All of these references to the diminutive, elfin music take on a greater significance: for Sheppard, the Chevalier's music is an extension of his ever euphonious inner life – 'And then the soul of all that scenery, the light of the fairy life, flashed back into his eyes; elfin-like in his jubilance, he clapped those little hands.'

In a similar way, Elise Polko's highly embroidered rehearings in 1869 of *Calm Sea and Prosperous Voyage* and *The Hebrides* only served to add layer upon layer of legend to Mendelssohn's life and work. In her half-literary, half-biographical *Reminiscences of Felix Mendelssohn-Bartholdy*, we encounter the remarkable fiction that Mendelssohn created the *Calm Sea and Prosperous Voyage* Overture just before departing for his first London sojourn, in 1829, 'a few days before the separation from his family, and for the consolation of his beloved and anxious mother'. Polko concocts a scene in which Mendelssohn plays the overture at the piano for his family before he leaves Berlin; and at the end of the work, 'the chorus joyfully sings – the loved one has reached the haven – Felix rises – the mother smiles, but tears stand in her fine eyes'.[2] And, after Felix's return from abroad, Polko weaves a similar scene for the creation of *The Hebrides*, complete with her own programmatic interpretation:

'The legend cannot be described by commonplace words, and you know that I am no poet; so I will play it over to you, and then you can tell me afterwards whether you saw and understood it all thoroughly.' Fair hands opened the well-loved instrument, and Mendelssohn played the wondrous legend subsequently called the 'Overture to the Hebrides'. For my part, I always seem, amid all its sportive strains, to see Mary Stuart's enticing, alluring eyes, as they looked forth in bygone days from the ivy-mantled windows of the Palace of Holyrood, when listening to the tones of her faithful minstrel Rizzio's lute.[3]

A generation later, the same qualities Elizabeth Sheppard had eulogized in the music of the Chevalier Seraphael – the free play of the imagination, the celebration of the fanciful – would be interpreted as a serious defect in Mendelssohn's music. In 1875, pondering the 'diversity of opinion with respect to Mendelssohn's merits', Friedrich Niecks assessed the music to *A Midsummer Night's Dream* to be the composer's 'most characteristic work and most successful achievement', in fact 'the result of his existence':

Mendelssohn opened a new world to the musician. Fairyland had not been a part of his domain – Mendelssohn conquered it for him. With the knavish sprite Puck, Peasblossom, Mustard-seed, Cobweb, and the lightsome throng of their nameless compatriots, we meet again and again in his works. The frolics of these merry sprites take in Mendelssohn's music the place which the purely human contents of Beethoven's scherzi hold in the latter composer's works. What is humour in Beethoven becomes fancy in Mendelssohn.[4]

For Niecks, Mendelssohn's music was like a mirror to the composer's 'harmonious inner life'. The predominance in his music of the 'fanciful', which Leigh Hunt had defined in 1844 as 'the youngest sister of Imagination without the other's weight of thought and feeling',[5] enabled Mendelssohn to gain in 'perspicuity, roundness of form, and serenity of aspect', but caused him nevertheless to lose in 'depth, height, and intensity'. Mendelssohn's music simply lacked the 'rugged energy, the subtle thoughtfulness and morbid world-weariness of other composers', whom Niecks likened to gladiators of modern times. And yet, Niecks found especially in Mendelssohn's overtures a 'centre of gravity':

Here he had a canvas allowing him full scope to display the luxurance of his fancy and excellence of his workmanship, give expression to his exquisite sympathy with nature, and yet not so large as to let the absence of the greater passions be too much felt. They [the overtures] represent most distinctly the imaginative element of his music. *Die Hebriden* is perhaps the best specimen of this kind of writing. In the overture to *A Midsummer Night's Dream*, the fanciful predominates.[6]

Along with a handful of other works (for example, the Octet; the Piano Trio in D minor, Op. 49, the Violin Concerto, Op. 64; and the *Italian* and *Scottish* Symphonies), our three overtures have remained a 'centre of gravity' for Mendelssohn's posthumous reputation. They stand in marked contrast, for example, to the changing receptions accorded *St Paul* and *Elijah*, in their time acknowledged for reestablishing the oratorio but at the close of the century heard by George Bernard Shaw as 'dreary fugue manufacturing' and 'oratorio mongering'; or to the *Lieder ohne Worte*, praised by Schumann for their romantic expression but sentimentalized after Mendelssohn's death by the addition of saccharine titles. In the main, the overtures have continued to receive critical approbation. They captured the essence of the romantic side of Mendelssohn's style, proved a decisive influence on the evolution of that style in the 1830s and 1840s (and on that of his contemporaries), and enjoyed a kind of compositional after-life later in the nineteenth century. In this chapter we shall consider certain aspects of their reception and influence.

The *Calm Sea and Prosperous Voyage* Overture offers a case in point. Though Mendelssohn drafted the work in 1828 and revised it extensively in 1834 before publishing it in 1835, he allowed an allusion to the opening contrabass motive to appear in print early in 1830 as the motto of 'Scheidend', the sixth song of the *Zwölf Lieder*, Op. 9. Here the motive is heard twice in the bass of the piano (bs 1 and 8, ex. 22). The rhythm is slightly adapted to fit the barcarolle-like $\frac{6}{8}$ metre of the song and, what is more, the motive is transposed up a step, from D to E major, but there can be little doubt that the motive is meant as a self-quotation, an explicit (at least to Mendelssohn) reference to the then unpublished overture.

As we know, the second theme of the overture served as a form of greeting between Mendelssohn and his friends, including Johann Gustav Droysen; indeed, it was Droysen who, using the pseudonym Voss, provided the verses for Op. 9 no. 6.[7] Appropriately, the poem concerns a journey in a skiff on a gentle sea, and the passage from youth to adulthood:

> Wie so gelinde die Fluth bewegt,
> Wie sie so ruhig den Nachen trägt.
> Fern liegt das Leben, das Jugendland,
> Fern liegt der Schmerz, der dort mich band,
> Sanft tragt mich Fluthen zum fernen Land!

(How gently flows the stream,/how quietly it carries the skiff./Far away is life, the land of youth,/far away is the pain that bound me there,/Bear me gently, stream, to a distant land!)

Mendelssohn composed his setting in Berlin on 13 January 1830,[8] not many weeks after he himself had returned from England. When Op. 9 was published, probably around March, in two groups of six, the composer placed the song at the conclusion of the first group, entitled 'The Youth' ('Der Jüngling').[9] 'Scheidend' continued to hold a special significance for Mendelssohn: in May 1830 he began his grand tour of Germany, Austria, Italy, and Switzerland, and in August, he took the trouble to copy the

Ex. 22 'Scheidend', Op.9 no. 6

song into the album of the Viennese antiquarian Aloys Fuchs, entitling it 'Auf der Fahrt' ('On the Journey').[10]

Some seventy years later, at the end of the nineteenth century, Mendelssohn's overture was revived again to symbolize a voyage. Elgar

Ex. 23 Elgar, *Enigma* Variations, 'Romanza' (XIII)

introduced the first phrase of the second theme from *Prosperous Voyage*
into the 'Romanza' (XIII) of the *Enigma* Variations (1899) (ex. 23). The
four-note phrase appears, with quotation marks, altogether three times in
the first clarinet, the first two times in A♭ major, the third in E♭ major,
thus a semitone *below* the dominant A major and *above* the tonic D major
of Mendelssohn's overture. But the theme is never heard in full, and the
recall of the phrase in flat keys creates a mysterious tonal distance between
the variation and the overture. After each quotation, Elgar departs further
from his source by modifying and redirecting the phrase, towards C minor,
F minor (where, in a memorable triple *piano* passage, it is intoned in the
low brass), and finally G minor. But he includes other touches that act to
strengthen the connection. Thus, he places the phrase in the clarinet, an
instrument used by Mendelssohn at appearances of the theme in the exposition and recapitulation of the overture. And, more subtly, Elgar accompanies
the phrase with a brooding, oscillating figure in the strings that spells a
first-inversion harmony, a slight destabilization of the phrase that perhaps
recalls Mendelssohn's carefully calculated employment of inversions in the
overture (see p. 58).

Elgar did not identify the friend 'pictured within' the thirteenth variation,
thereby leaving to posterity yet another riddle, but scholars are fairly
certain that she was Lady Mary Lygon, who undertook a sea voyage to

Australia in 1899 with her brother when he became the Governor of New South Wales.[11] According to Elgar the drum roll accompanying the quotation was meant to 'suggest the distant throb of the engines of a liner'. The use of asterisks instead of initials for the 'Romanza', and its placement before the finale (in which Elgar himself is pictured) have prompted speculation about a hidden content of the variation; arguing in 1956 against Lady Mary Lygon as the subject, Ernest Newman asserted that Elgar was 'here dwelling in imagination on somebody and something the parting from whom and which had at some time or other torn the very heart out of him'.[12] Be that as it may, the Mendelssohn quotation is the agent that creates the sense of nostalgia and distance (both temporal and spatial), so that the vaguely familiar is revived in a poignantly unfamiliar, fin de siècle context.

The fleeting echoes of *Calm Sea and Prosperous Voyage* – dampened in 'Scheidend' and the *Enigma* Variations to just two four-note motives – are in marked contrast to the celebrated 'reception' of the Overture to *A Midsummer Night's Dream* in Mendelssohn's 1843 incidental music, an extraordinary (unique?) revival of a masterpiece of a seventeen-year-old prodigy by a fully mature thirty-four-year-old composer at the height of his career. Understandably, such an event attracted considerable critical attention, and the intricate relationships between the two works raised several compositional and aesthetic issues: to what extent was Mendelssohn able to incorporate the overture of his youth, conceived as an autonomous, independent composition, into a new, dramatic context? To what extent was the incidental music dependent on or independent of the overture? To what extent did the incidental music mark an original contribution or a continuation of the capricious styles and gossamer textures of Mendelssohn's overture, a recovering, as Tovey put it, of 'the unperturbed instincts of his boyhood'?[13] And, finally, to what extent did the incidental music of 1843 alter Mendelssohn's interpretation of the play in the overture of 1826?

Friedhelm Krummacher has examined thoroughly how these and other issues were explored during the 1840s and 1850s by Robert Schumann, the Shakespearean scholar G. G. Gervinus, and Franz Liszt, with strikingly different results.[14] Reviewing a Leipzig performance of the incidental music in 1844,[15] Schumann observed that except for the overture, Mendelssohn's music provided 'only an accompaniment, ... a bridge between Bottom and Oberon, without which the passage across to the realm of the elves was quite impossible'. For Schumann, Mendelssohn had concentrated primarily on music for the fairies ('Feenparthien'), and, perhaps, had been too influenced by the overture, breaking off pieces of it for reemployment in the incidental music. A particular concern for Schumann was the conclusion of the work, in which the fairies' music was brought back from the overture more or less intact. Here, Schumann thought, Mendelssohn missed an opportunity to explore new musical terrain. Admittedly, the composer's intention had been to ensure the rounding off of the whole ('Abrundung des Ganzen'); still, 'if only Mendelssohn had again composed for this place something new!' Nevertheless, despite its reliance on the overture, and its elevation of the fairies (Schumann would have preferred additional numbers for the lovers), Mendelssohn's music was 'elegant and spirited enough'.

In the view of G. G. Gervinus, whose criticism was levied as much against Ludwig Tieck's 1843 production of the play as against the incidental music, Mendelssohn misconstrued Shakespeare and needlessly prolonged the action of the play by introducing an untimely, unnecessarily delaying form of musical accompaniment.[16]

How can one cross such an individual, fantastic work with such far too unsophisticated a composition? How can one disturb such a light and refined play, such an ethereal dream-creation, with the uncouth noise of a march with drums and trumpets, especially where Theseus expresses himself about these ethereal apparitions?

Thus, in contrast to Schumann, Gervinus found Mendelssohn's music – specifically the wedding march – too heavy-handed, too demanding, a charge he presumably would have applied to the rich content of the overture as well.

But for Franz Liszt, who conducted the *Midsummer Night's Dream* music in Weimar on 1 April 1854 and then published an article in response to Gervinus in the *Neue Zeitschrift für Musik*,[17] Mendelssohn had chosen with unfailing discretion just those moments in the play that could be enhanced by music. Liszt found in Shakespeare's play the blending of three quite different elements – the sentimental, the fantastic, and the comical. Mendelssohn's genius (admittedly, a 'less titanic genius than Beethoven, but a composer equipped with a most tender, sensitive, and completely cultured intelligence') was to weld these heterogeneous elements into a unified whole. In particular, according to Liszt, the overture

soars to the very height of poetry through its piquant originality, proportion, and euphony in the organic fusing of heterogeneous elements, and through its charm and freshness. One thinks only of the wind chords at the beginning and end! Do they not resemble slowly drooping and rising eyelids, between which is depicted a charming dream-world of the most lovely contrasts? In these contrasts are met those elements (sketched above) of the sentimental, fantastic, and comical, each one of which is masterfully characterized and yet entwined together with delicate, beautiful threads.[18]

Three years before, in 1851, Liszt himself had paid homage to Mendelssohn by publishing with Breitkopf & Härtel a transcription of the wedding march and fairies' music for piano solo (*Hochzeitsmarsch und Elfenreigen*, Searle 410). It is, perhaps, appropriate that Liszt chose to focus his arrangement on the march, the very piece that Gervinus found so offensive (*Marschlärm*); indeed, Liszt played to the hilt those noisy trumpets, specifying 'marcata quasi Tromba la melodia'. Much of the transcription follows fairly faith-fully the structure of Mendelssohn's original – a recurring C-major march theme with two contrasting trios – but Liszt indulges in some notable revisions. First, he works in several additional statements of the march theme, to permit a full display of virtuoso effects, including the three-hand technique, and an especially bombastic statement with full chords for both hands. Then, with the first trio – given in A♭ major instead of the dominant G – Liszt departs further from his model. The second trio appears in the 'correct' key of F major, but, just at the moment the C major march refrain should return, the trio is interrupted by an unexpected turn to B major and a capricious cadenza, Liszt's preparation for the 'Elfenreigen', which now begins in earnest in E minor, with a faithful transcription of the music from bs 8–57 of the overture (Ex. 24a). A brief cadenza-like flourish on the dominant of E minor leads us back to the C major march, to a new series of brilliant variations, and, finally, to the coda and conclusion of the

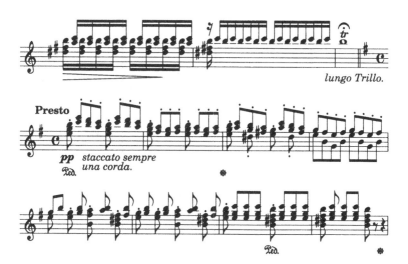

Ex. 24a Liszt, *Hochzeitsmarsch und Elfenreigen* (S 410)

97

Ex. 24b *A Midsummer Night's Dream* incidental music, Op. 61 no. 12

march. As Liszt no doubt recognized, Mendelssohn's march offered a clear enough link to the fairies' music: the melody begins off the tonic with a gesture to E minor before C major is affirmed. Mendelssohn himself took advantage of this detail to link the march and the fairy music from the overture, at the moment the wedding train exits in No. 12 of the incidental music and Puck enters for the finale (Ex. 24b). Very likely this interruption, a point of contact between the sentimental and the fantastic, provided Liszt with the idea for his transcription.

Well before Schumann's 1844 observation that the music to *A Midsummer Night's Dream* was 'elegant and spirited enough', Mendelssohn had thoroughly incorporated the scherzo-like character of the overture into his mature style. As we saw in Chapter 1, the scherzo of the Octet provided an important preliminary study for the ethereal textures of the overture, and, indeed, two other works from 1825 – the Capriccio in F♯ minor for piano, Op. 5, and the scherzo of the B-minor Piano Quartet, Op. 3 – also offered precedents. But it was *A Midsummer Night's Dream* Overture that spawned a proliferation of scherzo textures in a wide range of Mendelssohn's music.

Thus, in a setting of Heinrich Heine's 'Neue Liebe', which appeared in 1833 as the fourth song of the *Sechs Gesänge*, Op. 19a, Mendelssohn found an opportunity to revive the diminutive style of the overture. In a moonlit forest a wanderer encounters a procession of elves led by a queen. Does her beguiling smile symbolize his new love or presage his death? For this interaction between a mortal and elves Mendelssohn devised a delicate, staccato setting in F♯ minor, with a descending tetrachord not far removed from that of the overture (Ex. 25).

A Midsummer Night's Dream exercised a more general influence on a variety of Mendelssohn's instrumental works, including the Scherzo in

B minor (1829); *Rondo capriccioso*, Op. 14; Caprice, Op. 16 no. 2; and *Scherzo a capriccioso* for piano (1836), as well as several chamber works, among them the scherzos of the two Piano Trios, Opp. 49 and 66, and the String Quartet, Op. 44 no. 2; and, of the orchestral works, the finale of the Violin Concerto, Op. 64. Indeed, the specialized type of light scherzo

Ex. 25 'Neue Liebe', Op. 19a no. 4

came to be seen as an integral part of the composer's style; it was here, in Liszt's view, that Mendelssohn's talent readily took flight in a serenely 'entranced and entrancing atmosphere'.[19]

Not surprisingly, other composers imitated the Mendelssohnian scherzo. As early as 1833, in the E major overture to his second opera, *Die Feen*, the young Richard Wagner included a striking progression of wind chords likely inspired by the overture to *A Midsummer Night's Dream* (Ex. 26).

Ex. 26 Wagner, *Die Feen* Overture

The scherzos of Robert Schumann's three String Quartets, Op. 41 (1842, dedicated to Mendelssohn), have a *Märchenhaft* quality not unlike that of the *A Midsummer Night's Dream*, and, much later in the century, the scherzo of Richard Strauss's youthful Piano Sonata Op. 3 (1881) betrays a suspicious stylistic nod towards Mendelssohn.[20] In the first act of Gounod's *Roméo et Juliette* (1867) the 'Ballade of Queen Mab', who 'presides over dreams, lighter than the wind' ('préside aux songes, plus légère que le vent'), is a not too distant relative of Mendelssohn's overture, though its brisk E major chromatic figuration recalls too the *Rondo capriccioso* (Berlioz's extraordinary scherzo in his *Roméo et Juliette*, 'La reine Mab ou la fée des songes' – 'Queen Mab or the Fairy of Dreams' – utilizes sustained wind chords and violins divided *a 4*, but apparently was written *before* he heard Mendelssohn's *A Midsummer Night's Dream*.[21]) An imitation by an epigone of Mendelssohn occurs in the fifth movement of Niels Gade's *Elverskud*, Op. 30 (*The Erlking's Daughter*, 1853), in which Lord Oluf is seduced by elves in a forest on the eve of his wedding. Rather unambiguously, the music points to the overture of Gade's mentor, under whom the Danish composer served in Leipzig at the Gewandhaus during the 1840s. Thus Gade's music commences in E minor but changes to the major mode at the entrance of the elves' chorus and features a thinned-out texture for muted violins and sustained wind.

If, as Niecks asserted, in *A Midsummer Night's Dream* Mendelssohn conquered the fanciful, a quality we indeed encounter often in his music, in *The Hebrides* Overture he explored the exotic, again with lasting repercussions for his own work and for German musical romanticism. Elsewhere I have argued that we may distinguish in Mendelssohn's *œuvre* a Scottish (Ossianic) manner characterized by open-spaced sonorities, pentatonic and modal divisions of the octave, unusual (for Mendelssohn) parallelisms in voice leading, and, in general, an attempt to capture a certain unrefined, spontaneous sound quality.[22]

Though the first indications of this style were already stirring in the *Phantasie (Sonate écossaise)*, Op. 28, evidently conceived *before* Mendelssohn's Scottish tour, the full implications of the Scottish manner emerged first in *The Hebrides*. The other major work conceived in Scotland, the *Scottish* Symphony, forms an instructive parallel to the overture: at the end of July, just a few days before his visit to western Scotland, Mendelssohn sketched in Edinburgh the germinal ideas for the first movement of the symphony,[23] and here we find already the sequential, three-tiered motivic construction similar to that at the beginning of the overture (Ex. 27). But Mendelssohn allowed the symphony to gestate slowly: fully thirteen years elapsed between the sketch of 1829 and the first performance of the completed symphony in 1842. By 1835, the composer had finally released the overture as the first musical response to his impressions of Scotland. In a way, the *Scottish* Symphony thus stands in relation to *The Hebrides* as does the incidental music to *A Midsummer Night's Dream* to its overture: in

Ex. 27 *Scottish* Symphony, Op. 56

each case, an overture of the youthful prodigy influenced profoundly a major work of the artist in his prime.

It is not surprising, then, to detect in the symphony several echoes of *The Hebrides* Overture. There is no question here of direct borrowing of material, as in the case of Op. 61 from Op. 21. Moreover, there is probably no issue here of an Ossianic programmatic content; as we know, Mendelssohn sketched the opening ideas for the symphony after he visited Holyrood Palace and its chapel in Edinburgh where Mary reigned as Queen of Scotland after 1561. As if heeding Schumann's suggestion, Mendelssohn indeed composed something new in the symphony. But its general style and tone, especially that of the first movement, are indebted to the overture in several ways. Thus, there is the distinctive, dark scoring of the opening introduction, with the theme entrusted to the violas and oboes (compare, in *The Hebrides*, the initial use of low strings and bassoons). In addition, the thematic ingredients of the exposition (now expanded to three thematic groups) derive organically from the material of the introduction (note, too, how the first theme serves as accompaniment to the second thematic idea in b. 125, a technique similar to the linking of theme and accompaniment in the overture). Finally, we might mention the use of empty, open-spaced sonorities, and, at the close of the exposition and beginning of the development, the unconventional voice-leading and harmonic progressions that transport us from the dominant E directly to C♯ minor, B minor, and C minor.

Mendelssohn's Scottish manner experienced another revival in 1846, late in the composer's career, when he composed the still unpublished concert scene for bass and orchestra, *On Lena's Gloomy Heath*. The work was written for the Englishman Henry Phillips, who selected two passages from the third and fourth books of Macpherson's *Fingal*.[24] Here the slumbering Ossian is summoned by a vision of his deceased wife, Everallin, to rise and save their son, Oscar, ambushed by the sons of Lochlin. Mendelssohn devised a tripartite structure for the piece: an introduction to set the dark mood, a recitative-like transition for Everallin's dramatic plea, and a spirited march to accompany Ossian's preparations for battle. Not surprisingly, the style and atmosphere of *On Lena's Gloomy Heath*, in which we encounter again dark scorings, widely spaced sonorities, and quasi-pentatonic divisions of the octave (see Ex. 28a), recall *The Hebrides* Overture, and provide, finally, a direct link between Mendelssohn and Ossian.

At least one passage in *On Lena's Gloomy Heath* is remarkably close to another Ossianic work, the *Nachklänge von Ossian* (*Echoes of Ossian*, 1840) of

Ex. 28a *On Lena's Gloomy Heath*

Niels Gade (Ex. 28b–c). Here we come full circle to *The Hebrides* Overture, for Gade's youthful work, his Op. 1, is musically indebted to Mendelssohn's overture on several counts.[25] For Gade, as for Julius Benedict, *The Hebrides* (*Fingal's Cave*) Overture carried Ossianic connotations.[26] Nor was Gade alone in sustaining the interest of composers in Ossian settings. The young Brahms included two examples, a *Gesang aus Fingal* in his *Gesänge für Frauenchor*, Op. 17 (1860), and *Darthulas Grabesgesang*, Op. 42 no. 3 (1861), for six-part *a cappella* choir. In the understated *Gesang aus Fingal*, a modest setting for female chorus, two horns, and harp (the instrument associated with the bard), Brahms sought to explore in his own way something of the primitive, exotic qualities captured earlier by Mendelssohn.[27]

All three overtures thus generated *Nachklänge* during the nineteenth century, and continued to resonate in the nineteenth-century critical tradition. By publishing the overtures as a triptych in 1835, and by thus stressing

Ex. 28b *On Lena's Gloomy Heath*

Ex. 28c Gade, *Nachklänge von Ossian*, Op. 1

their aesthetic and stylistic commonalities, Mendelssohn surely recognized their special position in his art. During the late 1820s and early 1830s, the concert overture, in short, was the fertile testing ground for Mendelssohn's own, highly individualistic approach to programmatic music. Shakespeare, Goethe, and a multitude of Scottish impressions served to inspire his most romantic muse: here literary, visual, and purely musical images freely co-mingled, forming in Mendelssohn's imagination an expressive, 'characteristic' language for which, as he would have argued, words indeed remain inadequate.

Notes

1 Background

1 In a conversation between Wagner and Edward Dannreuther. Quoted in Dannreuther's Wagner article for Sir George Grove's *Dictionary of Music and Musicians*, vol. 4 (London, 1893), p. 369.

2 In *The World* (1 June 1892), included in *Shaw's Music: The Complete Musical Criticism*, ed. D. Laurence (London, 1981), vol. 2, p. 632.

3 *Neue Zeitschrift für Musik* 3 (1835), 127; trans. in Robert Schumann, *On Music*, p. 219.

4 On the evolution of the programme for the *Symphonie fantastique*, see Nicholas Temperley, 'The *Symphonie fantastique* and its program', *The Musical Quarterly* 57 (1971), 593–608. For Mendelssohn's unusually harsh criticism of Berlioz's symphony, expressed privately in a letter to his mother of 15 March 1831, see *Reisebriefe von 1830/31*, pp. 210–11 (also p. 85 below). The passage was deleted in the *Reisebriefe* prepared by the composer's brother Paul (Leipzig, 1861).

5 *Briefe aus den Jahren 1830 bis 1847*, vol. 2 pp. 221–2. See p. 70 below.

6 On 28 October 1818, at a concert given by the hornist Friedrich Gugel. See Rudolf Elvers, 'Ein Jugendbrief von Felix Mendelssohn', in *Festschrift für Friedrich Smend zum 70. Geburtstag* (Berlin, 1963), pp. 95–7.

7 See further R. Larry Todd, *Mendelssohn's Musical Education*, pp. 12–15.

8 *Letters of Felix Mendelssohn to Ignaz and Charlotte Moscheles*, p. 1.

9 See Todd, *Mendelssohn's Musical Education*, passim.

10 In J. C. Lobe, 'Gespräche mit Felix Mendelssohn', *Fliegende Blätter für Musik* 1/5 (1855), 280–96, in *Mendelssohn and His World*, ed. R. Larry Todd, p. 198.

11 See Sebastian Hensel, *The Mendelssohn Family (1729–1847)*, vol. 1, pp. 121–2.

12 According to A. B. Marx the *sinfonie* were performed with Mendelssohn providing a continuo accompaniment at the keyboard, after baroque practice. See A. B. Marx, *Erinnerungen aus meinem Leben* (Berlin, 1865), in *Mendelssohn and His World* (see p. 207). On Mendelssohn's interest in the 'Jupiter' Symphony, see my 'Mozart according to Mendelssohn: a contribution to *Rezeptionsgeschichte*', in *Perspectives on Mozart Performance*, ed. R. Larry Todd and Peter Williams (Cambridge, 1991), pp. 162–70.

13 *Allgemeine musikalische Zeitung* 30 (1828), 63.

14 See further my 'A Mendelssohn miscellany' and the literature cited therein. Mendelssohn also used the device of recalling material in finales in his Sextet, Op. 110, and Piano Sonata in B♭ major, Op. 106.

15 Hensel, vol. 1, p. 131.

16 'Frosch im Laub und Grill im Gras,/Verfluchte Dilettanten!/Fliegenschnauz und Mückennas,/Ihr seid doch Musikanten!' *Goethe's Faust*, trans. Walter Kaufman (New York, 1963), p. 397. In March 1832 the scherzo of the Octet was performed in Paris in a memorial mass for Beethoven, and Mendelssohn, struck by the peculiar choice of music, reported: 'While the priest was officiating at the altar during the scherzo, it really sounded like "Fliegenschnauz und Mückennas, verfluchte Dilettanten". The people, however, con-

sidered it very fine sacred music.' See his letter of 31 March 1832 in *Briefe aus den Jahren 1830 bis 1847* (henceforth *Briefe*), vol. 1, pp. 260–1.

17 Eduard Devrient, *My Recollections of Felix Mendelssohn-Bartholdy*, pp. 22–3.

18 *Berliner allgemeine musikalische Zeitung* 4 (1827), 288.

2 Genesis

1 New York Public Library, Mendelssohn Family Correspondence.

2 August Wilhelm Schlegel, *Shakespeares dramatische Werke*. Mendelssohn's aunt, Dorothea Veit, married Schlegel's brother Friedrich and in 1808 converted to Catholicism with him.

3 On Tieck's role in the Shakespeare edition, see Roger Paulin, *Ludwig Tieck*, pp. 253ff.

4 For a brief consideration of Tieck's role in the production, see Paulin, pp. 336–8.

5 Hensel, vol. 1, p. 130. Mendelssohn himself executed some drawings of the garden house and surrounding grounds. See Cécile Lowenthal-Hensel, 'Neues zur Leipziger Strasse Drei', in *Mendelssohn Studien*, vol. 7 (Berlin, 1990), pp. 144–5.

6 Marx, *Erinnerungen aus meinem Leben*, vol. 2, p. 229; from the translation by Susan Gillespie in *Mendelssohn and His World*, pp. 216–17.

7 By 1839 Mendelssohn and Marx had ended their friendship; Marx destroyed Mendelssohn's letters to him.

8 M. Deneke Mendelssohn Collection, b. 5, fols 7–12v.

9 It was performed with the *Jubel* Cantata, although there was no musical link between the two. See John Warrack, *Carl Maria von Weber*, p. 187. The overture concludes with a version of *God Save the King*, taken over by Weber from his earlier cantata written after the Battle of Waterloo, *Kampf und Sieg*.

10 It forms vol. 32 of the Mendelssohn Nachlass, which was deposited during the 1870s in the Deutsche Staatsbibliothek, Berlin. By 1833 Mendelssohn evidently had given the manuscript to A. B. Marx. See the composer's letter of 6 March 1833 to Breitkopf & Härtel, in Mendelssohn, *Briefe an deutsche Verleger*, p. 27.

11 Sibyl Marcuse, *Musical Instruments: A Comprehensive Dictionary* (New York, 1975), p. 43.

12 Composed at Bad Dobberan ca. July 1824. In a letter of 21 July 1824 to his sisters (New York Public Library), Mendelssohn offered a drawing and description of the bass horn: 'That is a large brass instrument that has a pretty, deep tone, and looks like a watering can or a syringe' ('Das ist ein grosses Instrument von Blech, hat einen schönen, tiefen Ton, und sieht so aus wie eine Giesskanne oder eine Spritze').

13 On the use of the bass horn, ophicleide, and serpent in German nineteenth-century music, see Michael Nagy, 'Der Serpent und seine Verwendung in der Musik der deutschen Romantik', in *Bläserklang und Blasinstrumente im Schaffen Richard Wagners*, ed. Wolfgang Suppan (Tutzing, 1985), pp. 49–72.

14 See n. 6; Devrient, p. 32; W. A. Lampadius, *Mendelssohn*, p. 44.

15 Lampadius, p. 44; Moscheles, *Recent Music and Musicians*, ed. Charlotte Moscheles, p. 89.

16 'Felix Mendelssohn-Bartholdy in Stettin', *Berliner allgemeine musikalische Zeitung* 4 (1827), p. 84 (14 March). Mendelssohn participated in the concert by performing one of his double piano concertos with Loewe. It is likely that the Kraków autograph, which contains rehearsal letters, was used for the performance of the overture.

17 Ferdinand Hiller, *Mendelssohn: Letters and Recollections*, p. 11.

18 *Bref till Adolf Fredrik Lindblad*, ed. L. Dahlgren, p. 26.

19 Lampadius, pp. 85–6. On 24 June Mendelssohn performed Beethoven's 'Emperor' Concerto; on both occasions he conducted the overture with a baton. See Mendelssohn's letters of 10, 16, and 17 July 1829 in Hensel, vol. 1, pp. 190–5. According to Sir George Grove, after the concert of 24 June, Mendelssohn's manuscript was 'left in a hackney coach and irrecoverably lost' (*A Dictionary of Music and Musicians*, vol. 2 (London, 1890), p. 328). But Mendelssohn's

autograph has indeed survived, and there does not seem to be firm documentation for Grove's anecdote.

20 *Harmonicon* 7 (1829), 204.

21 M. B. Foster, *History of the Philharmonic Society of London: 1813–1912* (London, 1912), p. 100. Smart conducted the overture from a copy given to him by Mendelssohn in November 1829; see H. B. and C. L. E. Cox, *Leaves from the Journals of Sir George Smart* (London, 1907; repr. New York, 1971), p. 271. The copy is now in the Royal Academy of Music, London (Ms. 2).

22 Letter of 21 February 1832, in *Briefe*, vol. 1, p. 254; Hiller, pp. 20–1.

23 *Franz Liszts Briefe*, ed. La Mara, vol. 3: *An eine Freundin*, p. 110.

24 For a review of this 'fiasco', see Judith Silber Ballan, 'Mendelssohn and the *Reformation* Symphony', pp. 47–8.

25 *Revue musicale* 12 (1832), 29 (25 February). Curiously, Mendelssohn's overture was otherwise ignored by the French press, possibly in retaliation to his critical comments about the St Simonian sect, then becoming a *cause célèbre* in Paris. See Adolphe Jullien, 'Mendelssohn à Paris', in *Airs variés* (Paris, 1877), pp. 106–8; on Mendelssohn's relations with the St Simonians, see Ralph P. Locke, 'Mendelssohn's collision with the St. Simonians', in *Mendelssohn and Schumann: Essays on Their Music and Its Context*, ed. J. W. Finson and R. Larry Todd, pp. 109–22.

26 *Harmonicon* 7 (1829), 193, 242. For a summary of the affair see Eric Werner, *Mendelssohn: A New Image*, pp. 153–4.

27 New York Public Library, Mendelssohn Family Correspondence.

28 See *Harmonicon* 10 (1832), 152; Lampadius, p. 193; and *Briefe an deutsche Verleger*, pp. 12–13, 16.

29 Folger Shakespeare Library, Washington D. C., Ms. V.a. 372 [olim 6256]. This manuscript was evidently prepared between March and July 1832; in a letter of 28 February to his parents Mendelssohn notes 'dann muss ich die Ouvertüre zum Sommernachtstraum 4händig arrangiren'. The 1832 arrangement was probably based on an earlier one used by Felix and Fanny for their 1826 duet performance before Moscheles. Curiously, the Folger autograph is barred in common time (with the fairies' music in semiquavers) and has the tempo marking Allegro vivace. On the upper right-hand corner of the title page appears the date '10th July', and beneath this, in a second hand, the erroneous year '1829'. As late as 4 July 1832 Mendelssohn sent several corrections for the arrangement to Karl Klingemann in London (*Felix Mendelssohn-Bartholdys Briefwechsel mit Legationsrat Karl Klingemann*, ed. K. Klingemann, p. 95).

30 *Allgemeine musikalische Zeitung* 34 (1832), 863–4; 35 (1833), 201–4. Breitkopf & Härtel also issued at this time an arrangement for solo piano by F. Mockwitz. In the *Katalog des Archivs von Breitkopf & Härtel*, no. 63, Wilhelm Hitzig lists an autograph arrangement by Mendelssohn of the overture for piano two hands, but there is no evidence in Mendelssohn's correspondence that he ever prepared such an arrangement.

31 *Harmonicon* 11 (1833), 146.

32 *Iris im Gebiete der Tonkunst* 3/47 (1832), 187.

33 *Allgemeine musikalische Zeitung* 35 (1833), cols. 23, 61, 195–6.

34 Ibid., col. 180.

35 *Briefe an deutsche Verleger*, p. 26.

36 Ibid., pp. 31–2, 33–4, 35–6, 37.

37 *Allgemeine musikalische Zeitung* 37 (1835), cols. 294–6.

38 *Berliner allgemeine musikalische Zeitung* 1 (1824), 391–6.

39 See chapter 1, n. 14.

40 A. B. Marx, 'Etwas über die Symphonie und Beethovens Leistungen in diesem Fache', *Berliner allgemeine musikalische Zeitung* 1 (1824), 174.

41 See Judith Silber Ballan, 'Marxian programmatic music', pp. 155ff; also, pp. 76 below.
42 Klingemann, p. 49.
43 Letter to Fredrik Lindblad, *Bref*, p. 24.
44 A. B. Marx, *Über Malerei in der Tonkunst*, p. 60.
45 Hensel, vol. 1, p. 161.
46 Devrient, p. 45; G. Droysen, 'Johann Gustav Droysen und Felix Mendelssohn-Bartholdy',
    p. 116. According to this account the head motive of the second theme of *Prosperous Voyage*,
    scored for cello, became a form of greeting between the friends.
47 Klingemann, pp. 52–3; Devrient, p. 81. The first Philharmonic performance, however, did
    not occur until 22 February 1836 (Foster, p. 137).
48 Letter to Fredrik Lindblad, *Bref*, p. 31.
49 Julius Schubring, 'Reminiscences of Felix Mendelssohn-Bartholdy', in *Mendelssohn and
    His World*, p. 229.
50 *Allgemeine musikalische Zeitung* 35 (1833), 59.
51 Devrient, p. 174.
52 New York Public Library, Mendelssohn Family Correspondence.
53 M. Deneke Mendelssohn Collection, b. 5, fols 13–16v. Conceivably these pages may have come
    to form part of vol. 16 of the Mendelssohn Nachlass, a volume retained by Mendelssohn's
    heirs when the Nachlass was sold to the Königliche Bibliothek in Berlin in 1878. See Rudolf
    Elvers, 'Auf den Spuren der Autographen von Felix Mendelssohn Bartholdy', pp. 83–91.
54 *Briefe an deutsche Verleger*, p. 33.
55 For a description, see *The Mary Flagler Cary Music Collection*, ed. Charles Ryskamp (New
    York, 1970), p. 34.
56 Klingemann, p. 131; *Briefwechsel zwischen Felix Mendelssohn Bartholdy und Julius Schubring*,
    p. 81.
57 *Allgemeine musikalische Zeitung* 36 (1834), cols. 302–3, 780; Alfred Dörffel, *Geschichte der
    Gewandhausconcerte zu Leipzig vom 25. November 1781 bis 25. November 1881* (Leipzig,
    1884), p. 83.
58 *Briefe an deutsche Verleger*, p. 40; Mendelssohn's corrected proofs for the score are in the
    Museum für Geschichte der Stadt Leipzig. See *Felix Mendelssohn Bartholdy–Autographen,
    Erstausgaben, Frühdrucke*, ed. Peter Krause, p. 55.
59 *Briefe an deutsche Verleger*, pp. 45, 46; *Allgemeine musikalische Zeitung* 37 (1835), 604.
60 Robert Schumann, *Neue Zeitschrift für Musik* 3 (1835), 127. See also Mendelssohn's letter
    of 6 October 1835 to his family in Berlin, in *Briefe*, vol. 1, p. 64.
61 Mendelssohn's and Klingemann's Scottish tour has been carefully reconstructed by Roger
    Fiske in *Scotland in Music*; see especially pp. 132ff.
62 Hensel, vol. 1, pp. 205–6.
63 For further analysis of the sketch, including the parallel motion of the opening bars and
    Gounod's comment in source no. 5, see my 'Of sea gulls and counterpoint', pp. 199–202.
64 Hensel, vol. 1, p. 204. In a letter of 1 December 1829, written after he had crossed the
    English Channel, Mendelssohn reported to Klingemann that he had again become indis-
    posed, and had closed his eyes as he had during the trip to Staffa (Klingemann, p. 65).
65 Hensel, vol. 1, p. 205.
66 According to an inaccurate account recorded by Ferdinand Hiller, recalling his 1832
    conversation about the overture with Mendelssohn in Paris: 'He told me that not only was
    its general form and colour suggested to him by the sight of Fingal's Cave, but that the
    first few bars, containing the principal subject, had actually occurred to him on the spot.
    The same evening he and his friend Klingemann paid a visit to a Scotch family. There
    was a piano in the drawing-room, but being Sunday, music was utterly out of the
    question, and Mendelssohn had to employ all his diplomacy to get the instrument opened
    for a single minute, so that he and Klingemann might hear the theme which forms the

germ of that original and masterly Overture, which, however, was not completed till some years later at Düsseldorf' (Hiller, pp. 18–19). Sunday would have fallen on 9 August, the morning when the travellers returned to Oban.

67 *Briefe aus Leipziger Archiven*, pp. 126–31; Klingemann, pp. 82–4; New York Public Library, Mendelssohn Family Correspondence.

68 Letter in the New York Public Library, Mendelssohn Family Correspondence.

69 Ibid.

70 See my 'Of sea gulls and counterpoint', pp. 204–13.

71 Letters of 16 October and 16, 23, and 30 November 1830 in *Briefe*, vol. 1, pp. 31, 46, 48, and 52.

72 Ibid., p. 60.

73 M. Deneke Mendelssohn Collection, d. 58. It may have been intended for the violinist Eduard Rietz, to whom Mendelssohn had promised to send a copy of the overture on 30 November.

74 *Die Hebriden*, ed. Hugo von Mendelssohn-Bartholdy (Basel, 1947). For a description of the manuscript and its provenance, see Georg Kinsky, *Musikhistorisches Museum von Wilhelm Heyer in Köln*, vol. 4 (Cologne, 1916), pp. 330–3.

75 Berlioz, *Memoirs*, p. 293.

76 G. Abraham, 'The scores of Mendelssohn's "Hebrides"', *Monthly Musical Record* 78 (1948), 172–6.

77 'Mendelssohn's "Die einsame Insel"', *Music and Letters* 26 (1945), 148–50. Abraham mistakenly proposed that *Die einsame Insel* was 'in existence since, perhaps, the end of 1829'. Walker was under the false impression that the Bodleian copy of *Die einsame Insel* was in fact a Mendelssohn autograph.

78 *Briefe*, vol. 1, p. 241.

79 Hiller, pp. 18–19.

80 Moscheles, *Recent Music and Musicians*, pp. 178–9.

81 New York Public Library, Mendelssohn Family Correspondence.

82 Ibid., unpublished letter of 25 February 1831.

83 Letter of 11 May 1832 (New York Public Library); in Felix Mendelssohn, *A Life in Letters*, p. 184. In a diary entry for 6 May, Mendelssohn recorded that the overture was finished ('Ouv. fertig'; Bodleian Library, M. Deneke Mendelssohn Collection, g. 4, f. 2r).

84 Foster, p. 115.

85 Letter of 18 May 1832, *Briefe*, vol. 1, p. 264; *Harmonicon* 10 (1832), 154.

86 *Athenaeum*, 19 May 1832.

87 *Harmonicon* 10 (1832), 142. Significantly, there is no mention of Fingal's Cave in this review.

88 British Library Additional Ms. 33965, f. 251. Foster, p. 110.

89 *Catalogue of the Mendelssohn Papers in the Bodleian Library, Oxford*, vol. 3, p. 308; see also C. E. Horsley, 'Reminiscences of Mendelssohn by his English pupil', *Dwight's Journal of Music* 32 (1872), in *Mendelssohn and His World*, p. 237. According to his diary, the arrangement was finished as early as 5 June (M. Deneke Mendelssohn Collection, g. 4, f. 4r).

90 J. R. Sterndale Bennett, *The Life of William Sterndale Bennett* (Cambridge, 1907), p. 125. From Sterndale Bennett the Ms. passed to Prof. Thomas Case and Mr. T. G. Odling.

91 For a summary of these changes see E. Walker, 'Mendelssohn's "Die einsame Insel"', and Abraham.

92 *Allgemeine musikalische Zeitung* 35 (1833), 125.

93 Ibid., 196.

94 See Mendelssohn's letter of 18 September 1833 in *Briefe an deutsche Verleger*, pp. 30–1.

95 Ibid., p. 31.

96 *Allgemeine musikalische Zeitung* 36 (1834), cols. 428–9.

97 Ibid.

98 *Briefe an deutsche Verleger*, p. 40; *Gesammelte Schriften über Musik und Musiker von Robert Schumann*, ed. F. Gustav Jansen, vol. 1, p. 181n.

99 'More letters by Mendelssohn', *Dwight's Journal of Music* 31 (1871), 58.

100 Reviewed in *Allgemeine musikalische Zeitung* 37 (1835), 295–6.

3 Musical influences

1 *Berliner allgemeine musikalische Zeitung* 3 (1826), 246.

2 Ibid.

3 See Julius Benedict, *Sketch of the Life and Work*, pp. 7ff.

4 See my 'Piano music reformed', pp. 184, 210.

5 Julius Schubring, 'Reminiscences', in *Mendelssohn and His World*, p. 229.

6 In the late 1830s Mendelssohn himself considered an opera libretto by Planché on the subject of Edward III and the Siege of Calais, but the project never came to fruition. See J. R. Planché, *Recollections and Reflections* (London, 1872), vol. 1, pp. 279–316.

7 Georg Kinsky, 'Was Mendelssohn indebted to Weber?'

8 Grove, 'Mendelssohn', in *A Dictionary of Music and Musicians* (London, 1890), vol. 2, p. 328.

9 New York Public Library, Mendelssohn Family Correspondence.

10 See Clive Brown, *Spohr: A Critical Biography*, pp. 78, 80.

11 See chapter 1, n. 14.

12 Johann Christian Lobe, 'Gespräche mit Mendelssohn', in *Mendelssohn and His World*, p. 194.

13 On this point, see further Ludwig Finscher, 'Weber's *Freischütz*: conceptions and misconceptions', *Proceedings of the Royal Musical Association* 110 (1984), 88–90, and Michael C. Tusa, *Euryanthe and Carl Maria von Weber's Dramaturgy of German Opera* (Oxford, 1991), p. 31n.

14 Letter of 1 April 1825 from Mendelssohn to his family in Berlin (New York Public Library, Mendelssohn Family Correspondence).

15 Cf. chapter 2, n. 38.

16 J. F. Reichardt, *Goethes Lieder, Oden, Balladen, und Romanzen mit Musik*, vol. 1 (Leipzig, Breitkopf & Härtel, 1809).

17 Concerning the first version, D 216a, and Schubert's revisions, see Timothy L. Jackson, 'Schubert's revisions of *Der Jüngling und der Tod*, D 545a–b, and *Meeresstille*, D 216a–b', *The Musical Quarterly* 75 (1991), 350–5.

18 See chapter 2, n. 44.

19 By 1828, Mendelssohn would have known only two overtures to Beethoven's opera, the *Fidelio* overture and *Leonore* No. 3. *Leonore* No. 1 was published in 1838; and *Leonore* No. 2, performed by Mendelssohn in Leipzig in 1840, was published in 1842. See Mendelssohn's letter to Aloys Fuchs of 28 August 1835, in *Mendelssohn and His World*, p. 296.

20 See chapter 2, n. 78.

21 See especially Roger Fiske, *Scotland in Music*.

22 *Letters of Felix Mendelssohn to Ignaz and Charlotte Moscheles*, p. 11.

23 See Fanny's letters of 23 May and 4 June 1829 in *The Letters of Fanny Hensel to Felix Mendelssohn*, ed. Marcia Citron, pp. 41, 50.

24 Fiske, p. 141.

25 In 1839, however, Mendelssohn did arrange a series of 'Schottische National-Lieder' (they have been edited by Rudolf Elvers, Leipzig, 1977).

26 Letter of 28 July 1829 from Mendelssohn to his father. *Mendelssohn: A Life in Letters*, p. 80.

27 For a discussion of this repertory, see Francis Collinson, *The Traditional and National Music of Scotland* (London, 1966), pp. 35ff.

28 Hensel, vol. 1, pp. 213–14.

29 See R. Larry Todd, 'Mendelssohn's Ossianic manner', pp. 142–4.

4 Formal considerations: a synoptic overview

1 Berlioz, *Memoirs*, p. 294.
2 Letter of 9 July 1856, in *Letters of Franz Liszt*, vol. 1, pp. 273–4.
3 August Reissmann, *Felix Mendelssohn-Bartholdy: sein Leben und seine Werke* (Berlin, 1867), quoted in Lampadius, p. 57.
4 A diminished seventh superimposed above the dominant, a blended wind sonority similar to one Mendelssohn had used in *A Midsummer Night's Dream* (bs 39–40, 56–7).
5 Lampadius, pp. 57–8. See also chapter 5, p. 77.
6 See Todd, 'Of sea gulls and counterpoint'.

5 The overtures as programmatic music

1 Friedrich von Schlegel, *Das Athenäum* (Jena, 1798–1800), p. 320; trans. in *Music and Aesthetics in the Eighteenth and Early-Nineteenth Centuries*, ed. Peter le Huray and James Day (Cambridge, 1981), p. 247.
2 *Neue Zeitschrift für Musik* 2 (1835), 202.
3 Devrient, pp. 35–6.
4 See Silber Ballan, 'Marxian programmatic music', pp. 152ff; and Scott Burnham, 'Criticism, faith, and the *Idee*', 183–92. As Burnham observes, Beethoven himself followed Marx's work in the *Berliner allgemeine musikalische Zeitung*.
5 See further Silber Ballan, 'Mendelssohn and the *Reformation* Symphony', pp. 148–204.
6 *Briefe*, vol. 2, pp. 221–2.
7 Souchay's letter, dated 12 October 1842, has survived in the Green Books collection of Mendelssohn's correspondence in the M. Deneke Mendelssohn Collection at Oxford (vol. 16, no. 69).
8 Unpublished letter of 31 January 1833, Munich, Bayerische Staatsbibliothek.
9 See further my '"Gerade das Lied wie es dasteht"'.
10 Frederick Niecks, *Programme Music in the Last Four Centuries*, p. 164.
11 *Briefe an deutsche Verleger*, pp. 25–6. Letter of 15 February 1833.
12 Niecks, *Programme Music*, p. 173.
13 Several commentators have discussed the use of the tetrachord, including Eric Werner, who viewed it as a type of *Urlinie*. See Werner, *Mendelssohn: A New Image*, pp. 408–10.
14 See Schubring, 'Reminiscences', in *Mendelssohn and His World*, p. 225.
15 *Allgemeine musikalische Zeitung* 49 (1847), col. 37.
16 See Lawrence Kramer, *'Felix culpa'*, pp. 68ff.
17 Ibid., p. 70.
18 See chapter 2, n.44.
19 Schubring, 'Reminiscences', in *Mendelssohn and His World*, p. 233, n. 15.
20 G. Droysen, p. 116.
21 Ernst Pfundt, *Die Pauken: Eine Anleitung dieses Instrument zu erlernen* (Leipzig, 1849), p. 29.
22 *Signale für die musikalische Welt* 5 (1847), 35, signed 'W.L.' I am grateful to J. Michael Cooper for bringing this review to my attention.
23 Donald Tovey, *Essays in Musical Analysis*, p. 402.
24 See Leon Botstein, 'The aesthetics of assimilation and affirmation', pp. 26ff, for a compelling exploration of this line of interpretation.
25 See, for example, his description of a *tableau vivant* executed for the Crown Prince of Prussia in Düsseldorf in 1833. Letter of 26 October 1833, in *Briefe*, vol. 2, pp. 8–10.
26 Botstein, p. 27.

27 Edward Lockspeiser, *Music and Painting*, pp. 10–12.
28 Botstein, p. 26.
29 Cited in W. Jackson Bate, *Samuel Johnson* (New York, 1975), p. 521.
30 J. G. Sulzer, *Allgemeine Theorie der schönen Künste*, 2nd edn (Leipzig, 1793), vol. 3, p. 634.
31 Hensel, vol. 1, p. 205.
32 Washington Irving, 'Abbotsford', in *The Works of Irving* (London and New York, n.d.), vol. 3, p. 522.
33 Hensel, vol. 1, p. 200.
34 Klingemann, p. 45.
35 See Peter Ward Jones, 'The Library of Felix Mendelssohn Bartholdy', in *Festschrift Rudolf Elvers zum 60. Geburtstag*, ed. E. Herttrich and H. Schneider (Tutzing, 1985), pp. 303–4. The Scott volumes were probably acquired by Mendelssohn during the 1830s, after his trip to Scotland.
36 See especially, Paul M. Ochojski, '*Waverley* Über Alles', pp. 260–70.
37 Hensel, vol. 1, p. 207.
38 See further, Todd, 'Mendelssohn's Ossianic manner', pp. 144–5.
39 *The Musical World*, 20 November 1847, p. 734.
40 Stendhal, *Life of Rossini*, trans. R. N. Coe (Seattle, 1972), p. 387.
41 *Allgemeine musikalische Zeitung* 35 (1833), col. 125.
42 Benedict, *Sketch of the Life and Works*, p. 20.
43 See chapter 2, n. 98.
44 See also Todd, 'Mendelssohn's Ossianic manner', pp. 145–6.

6 Some thoughts on Mendelssohn's orchestration

1 *Reisebriefe von 1830/31*, p. 211.
2 Marx, *Erinnerungen aus meinem Leben*, in *Mendelssohn and His World*, p. 212.
3 Tovey, p. 410.
4 See further my 'Orchestral texture and the art of orchestration', in *The Orchestra: Origins and Transformations*, ed. Joan Peyser (New York, 1986), pp. 213–14.

7 Influence and reception of the overtures

1 Elizabeth Sara Sheppard, *Charles Auchester*, 3 vols. (London, 1853). See further E. D. Mackerness, 'Music and moral purity in the early Victorian era', *Canadian Music Journal* 4 (1960), 19ff. Sheppard's novel remained in print into the first few decades of the twentieth century.
2 Elise Polko, *Reminiscences of Felix Mendelssohn-Bartholdy: A Social and Artistic Biography*, trans. Lady Wallace (London, 1869; rep. 1987), p. 11.
3 Ibid., pp. 13–14. Polko appears to have confused *The Hebrides* with the *Scottish* Symphony, inspired by Mendelssohn's 1829 visit to Holyrood Palace in Edinburgh.
4 Friedrich Niecks, 'On Mendelssohn and some of his contemporary critics'.
5 Leigh Hunt, 'In answer to the question: What is poetry?' Introduction to *Imagination and Fancy* (London, 1844).
6 Niecks, 'On Mendelssohn and some of his contemporary critics'.
7 See Droysen, p. 194. Droysen's pseudonym is sometimes mistakenly confused with the poet Johann Heinrich Voss.
8 The autograph, entitled 'Scheidelied', is in Paris, Bibliothèque Nationale, Conservatoire Ms. 193.
9 The second half of the opus, nos. 7–12, entitled 'Das Mädchen', contained three settings by Mendelssohn's sister Fanny (nos. 7, 10, and 12). On the publication history of Op. 9, see *Briefe an deutsche Verleger*, pp. 279ff.

10 See Georg Kinsky, ed., *Manuskripte – Briefe – Dokumente von Scarlatti bis Stravinsky, Katalog der Musikautographen-Sammlung Louis Koch* (Stuttgart, 1953), p. 333. On Mendelssohn's dealings with Fuchs, see Eduard Hanslick, 'Letters from Felix Mendelssohn-Bartholdy to Aloys Fuchs', in *Mendelssohn and His World*, pp. 275–309.

11 J. N. Moore, *Edward Elgar: A Creative Life* (Oxford, 1984), pp. 263–4.

12 *Sunday Times* (18 November 1956). See also Michael Kennedy, *Portrait of Elgar* (Oxford, 1987), pp. 95ff.

13 Tovey, p. 407.

14 Friedhelm Krummacher, ' ". . . fein und geistreich genug" ', pp. 89–117.

15 'Der *Sommernachtstraum* (Brieflich)', *Neue Zeitschrift für Musik* 20 (1844), 6–7.

16 G. G. Gervinus, *Shakespeare* (Leipzig, 1850), vol. 1, pp. 363f.

17 'Über Mendelssohns Musik zum "Sommernachtstraum" ', *Neue Zeitschrift für Musik* 40 (1854), 233–7; repr. in Franz Liszt, *Gesammelte Schriften*, ed. L. Ramann (Leipzig, 1881; Hildesheim, 1978), vol. 3, pp. 37–47. On Liszt's personal relations with Mendelssohn see Wm. A. Little, 'Mendelssohn and Liszt', in *Mendelssohn Studies*, ed. R. Larry Todd (Cambridge, 1992), pp. 106–25.

18 Liszt, 'Über Mendelssohns Musik zum "Sommernachtstraum" ', 44–5.

19 Ibid., p. 45.

20 See R. Larry Todd, 'Strauss before Liszt and Wagner: some observations', in *Richard Strauss: New Perspectives on the Composer and His Work*, ed. Bryan Gilliam (Durham, N. C., 1992).

21 See Berlioz, *Memoirs*, p. 294n.

22 See my 'Mendelssohn's Ossianic manner'.

23 See Douglass Seaton, 'A draft for the exposition of the first movement of Mendelssohn's "Scotch" Symphony', *Journal of the American Musicological Society* 30 (1977), 129ff.

24 See my 'Mendelssohn's Ossianic manner', pp. 153ff.

25 Ibid., pp. 146ff.

26 See chapter 5, n. 42.

27 For a partial listing of other Ossianic works, see Fiske, pp. 175–6.

Select bibliography

Abraham, G. 'The scores of Mendelssohn's "Hebrides"', *Monthly Musical Record* 78 (1948), 172–6

Anon. 'More letters by Mendelssohn', *Dwight's Journal of Music* 31 (1871), 58

Benedict, J. *Sketch of the Life and Work of the Late Felix Mendelssohn Bartholdy* (London, 1850)

Bennett, J. R. Sterndale. *The Life of William Sterndale Bennett* (Cambridge, 1907)

Berlioz, H. *The Memoirs of Hector Berlioz*, ed. and trans. D. Cairns (London and New York, 1969)

Botstein, Leon. 'The aesthetics of assimilation and affirmation: reconstructing the career of Felix Mendelssohn', in *Mendelssohn and His World*, ed. R. L. Todd (Princeton, 1991), pp. 5–42

Brown, C. *Spohr: A Critical Biography* (Cambridge, 1984)

Burnham, S. 'Criticism, faith, and the *Idee*: A. B. Marx's early reception of Beethoven', *19th Century Music* 13 (1990), 183–92

Catalogue of the Mendelssohn Papers in the Bodleian Library, Oxford, vols. 1 and 2, ed. M. Crum (Tutzing, 1980 and 1983), vol. 3, ed. P. W. Jones (Tutzing, 1989)

Citron, M., ed. and trans. *The Letters of Fanny Hensel to Felix Mendelssohn* (Stuyvesant, New York, 1987)

Dahlgren, L., ed. *Bref till Adolf Fredrik Lindblad från Mendelssohn, . . . och andra* (Stockholm, 1913)

Devrient, E. *Meine Erinnerungen an Felix Mendelssohn-Bartholdy und seine Briefe an mich* (Leipzig, 1869); *My Recollections of Felix Mendelssohn-Bartholdy and His Letters to Me*, trans. N. Macfarren (London, 1869; repr. New York, 1972)

Droysen, G. 'Johann Gustav Droysen und Felix Mendelssohn-Bartholdy', *Deutsche Rundschau* 111 (1902), 107–26, 193–215, 386–408

Elvers, R. 'Auf den Spuren der Autographen von Felix Mendelssohn Bartholdy', in *Festschrift Franz Grasberger*, ed. G. Brosche (Tutzing, 1975), pp. 83–91

Finson, J. W. and Todd, R. Larry, eds. *Mendelssohn and Schumann: Essays on Their Music and Its Context* (Durham, N. C., 1984)

Fiske, R. *Scotland in Music: A European Enthusiasm* (Cambridge, 1983)

Hensel, S. *The Mendelssohn Family (1729–1847) from Letters and Journals*, trans. C. Klingemann (London, 1882), 2 vols.

Hiller, F. *Mendelssohn: Letters and Recollections*, trans. M. E. von Glehn (London, 1874; repr. New York, 1972)

Hitzig, W. *Katalog des Archivs von Breitkopf & Härtel* (Leipzig, 1925)

Jansen, F. G., ed. *Gesammelte Schriften über Musik und Musiker von Robert Schumann*, 4th Aufl. (Leipzig, 1891)

Kinsky, G. 'Was Mendelssohn indebted to Weber?', *Musical Quarterly* 19 (1933), 178–86

Klingemann, K., ed. *Felix Mendelssohn-Bartholdys Briefwechsel mit Legationsrat Karl Klingemann in London* (Essen, 1909)

Kramer, L. '*Felix culpa*: Goethe and the image of Mendelssohn', in *Mendelssohn Studies*, ed. R. L. Todd (Cambridge, 1992), pp. 64–79

Krause, P., ed. *Felix Mendelssohn Bartholdy – Autographen, Erstausgaben, Frühdrucke* (Leipzig, 1972)

Krummacher, F. '". . . fein und geistreich genug": Versuch über Mendelssohns Musik zum *Sommernachtstraum*', in *Das Problem Mendelssohn*, ed. C. Dahlhaus (Regensburg, 1974), pp. 89–117

Lampadius, W. A. *Life of Mendelssohn*, trans. W. L. Gage (Boston, 1872)

Letters of Franz Liszt, ed. La Mara, trans. C. Bache (London, 1894), vol. 1

Liszt, F. 'Über Mendelssohns Musik zum "Sommernachtstraum"', *Neue Zeitschrift für Musik* 40 (1854), 233–7

An eine Freundin (*Briefe*, vol. 3), ed. La Mara (Leipzig, 1894)

Lobe, J. C. 'Gespräche mit Felix Mendelssohn', *Fliegende Blätter für Musik* 1/5 (1855), 280–96; trans. in *Mendelssohn and His World* (Princeton, 1991)

Lockspeiser, E. *Music and Painting: A Study in Comparative Ideas from Turner to Schoenberg* (London, 1973)

Marx, A. B. *Über Malerei in der Tonkunst* (Berlin, 1828)

Erinnerungen aus meinem Leben, 2 vols. (Berlin, 1865); trans. in part in *Mendelssohn and His World* (Princeton, 1991)

Mendelssohn Bartholdy, F. *Briefe aus den Jahren 1830 bis 1847*, ed. P. Mendelssohn Bartholdy, 4th edn (Leipzig, 1878)

Die Hebriden, Facsimile, ed. H. von Mendelssohn-Bartholdy (Basel, 1947)

Reisebriefe von 1830/31, ed. P. Sutermeister (Zurich, 1949)

Briefe an deutsche Verleger, ed. R. Elvers (Berlin, 1968)

Briefe aus Leipziger Archiven, eds. H.-J. Rothe and R. Szeskus (Leipzig, 1971)

A Life in Letters, ed. R. Elvers, trans. C. Tomlinson (London and New York, 1986)

Moscheles, C., ed. *Aus Moscheles Leben* (Leipzig, 1872), trans. A. D. Coleridge as *Recent Music and Musicians* (New York, 1873; rep. 1970)

Moscheles, F. ed. and trans. *Letters of Felix Mendelssohn to Ignaz and Charlotte Moscheles* (Boston, 1888)

Niecks, F. 'On Mendelssohn and some of his contemporary critics', *Monthly Musical Record* 5 (1875), 162–4; repr. in *Mendelssohn and His World* (Princeton, 1991), pp. 382–9

Programme Music in the Last Four Centuries: A Contribution to the History of Musical Expression (London, 1907; repr. New York, 1969)

Ochojski, P. M. '*Waverley* über Alles – Sir Walter Scott's German reputation', in *Scott Bicentenary Essays*, ed. A. Bell (New York, 1973), pp. 260–70

Paulin, R. *Ludwig Tieck: A Literary Biography* (Oxford, 1985)

Schlegel, A. W. *Shakespeares dramatische Werke*, 9 vols. (Berlin, 1797–1810)

Schubring, J. 'Reminiscences of Felix Mendelssohn-Bartholdy', *Musical World* 31 (12 May 1866)

Schubring, J., ed. *Briefwechsel zwischen Felix Mendelssohn Bartholdy und Julius Schubring* (Leipzig, 1892); repr. in *Mendelssohn and His World*, ed. R. Larry Todd (Princeton, 1991)

Schumann, R. *On Music*, ed. K. Wolff, trans. P. Rosenfeld (Berkeley, 1983)

Silber Ballan, J. 'Mendelssohn and the *Reformation* Symphony: a critical and historical study' (Ph.D. diss., Yale University, 1987)

'Marxian programmatic music: a stage in Mendelssohn's musical development', in *Mendelssohn Studies*, ed. R. Larry Todd (Cambridge, 1992), pp. 149–61

Todd, R. Larry. 'Of sea gulls and counterpoint: The Early Versions of Mendelssohn's *Hebrides* Overture', *19th Century Music* 2 (1979), 197–213

Mendelssohn's Musical Education: A Study and Edition of His Exercises in Composition (Cambridge, 1983)

'Mendelssohn's Ossianic manner, with a new source – *On Lena's Gloomy Heath*', in *Mendelssohn and Schumann: Essays on Their Music and Its Context*, ed. J. W. Finson and R. Larry Todd, pp. 137–60

'Piano music reformed: the case of Felix Mendelssohn Bartholdy', in *Nineteenth-Century Piano Music*, ed. R. Larry Todd (New York, 1990), pp. 178–220

'A Mendelssohn miscellany', *Music and Letters* 71 (1990), 52–64

ed., *Mendelssohn and His World* (Princeton, 1991)

'"Gerade das Lied wie es dasteht": on text and meaning in Mendelssohn's *Lieder ohne Worte*', in *Musical Humanism and Its Legacy: Studies in the History of Music Theory*, ed. N. K. Baker (Stuyvesant, New York, 1992), pp. 355–79

Tovey, D. *Essays in Musical Analysis* (London, 1935–7; repr. as one vol. 1981)

Walker, E. 'Mendelssohn's "Die einsame Insel"', *Music and Letters* 26 (1945), 148–50

Warrack, J. *Carl Maria von Weber* (London and New York, 1968)

Werner, E. *Mendelssohn: A New Image of the Composer and His Age*, trans. Dika Newlin (London and New York, 1963)

Index